100 ACTING EX
FOR 8-18 YEAI

100 ACTING EXERCISES FOR 8–18 YEAR OLDS

Samantha Marsden

methuen | drama

LONDON • NEW YORK • OXFORD • NEW DELHI • SYDNEY

METHUEN DRAMA
Bloomsbury Publishing Plc
50 Bedford Square, London, WC1B 3DP, UK
1385 Broadway, New York, NY 10018, USA
29 Earlsfort Terrace, Dublin 2, Ireland

BLOOMSBURY, METHUEN DRAMA and the Methuen
Drama logo are trademarks of Bloomsbury Publishing Plc

First published in Great Britain 2019
Reprinted 2019 (four times), 2020, 2021

Cover image © Michelle Darwin, Burnley Youth Theatre

A catalogue record for this book is available from the British Library.

Library of Congress Cataloging-in-Publication Data
Names: Marsden, Samantha, author.
Title: 100 acting exercises for 8 - 18 year olds / Samantha Marsden.
Description: London, UK ; New York, NY : Methuen Drama, 2019. | Includes index.
Identifiers: LCCN 2018035205 | ISBN 9781350049949 (pb) |
ISBN 9781350049963 (ePDF) | ISBN 9781350049970 (epub)
Subjects: LCSH: Child actors. | Acting–Study and teaching.
Classification: LCC PN3157 .M36 2019 | DDC 792.02/8083–dc23
LC record available at https://lccn.loc.gov/2018035205

ISBN: PB: 978-1-3500-4994-9
ePDF: 978-1-3500-4996-3
eBook: 978-1-3500-4997-0

Typeset by Integra Software Services Pvt. Ltd.
Printed and bound in Great Britain

To find out more about our authors and books visit www.bloomsbury.com
and sign up for our newsletters.

For Ms Spencer, the English teacher
who taught me that being dyslexic didn't have to be a barrier
and that teachers can change lives.

CONTENTS

FOREWORD

You never stop learning. Reading these pages that are rich in exercises and guidance to help you learn your craft is testament to that. The question is, when can you *start* learning? Acting is such an instinctive craft that there simply are no rules as to when you start and when you finish. It's an ever-evolving skill but one that begins with observing and listening, certainly not showing and telling. From an early age, we all start inhabiting other people's mannerisms and characteristics: sadly some of these come back to haunt us when we realize we are becoming our parents! As soon as granny dribbles and drools over the cot, making baby noises at the infant, that same child soon retaliates with similar sounds and expressions. For me, those moments were probably the most coherent conversations I ever had with my grandmother, but that's enough self-realization from me. It is a pity our brains are not programmed to recall those first moments of primary communication, because in a very fundamental way they are our first acting lessons too. We listen, we observe and we respond with absolute pure intent: albeit that intention is invariably 'like me, feed me'. It is that first lesson in communication and that hunger to be liked which can often fuel the young wannabe actor to hone their craft. We are all a mixed bag of insecurities, and some of those insecurities are beautifully and sensitively broken down through games and exercises in this book to allow the actor to be less inhibited in the rehearsal room and more truthful in his or her performance. For directors, teachers, actors and students of life, this book helps you crack the code and have some fun along the way. I passionately believe in the values practical theatre learning can give to many a young and not-so-young person wherever his or her career path takes him or her. When I started my own theatre career, there was pressure to gain an equity card as soon as possible. Today the challenge is more fundamental; it is about gaining an empathy card, and the route to that is through curiosity and compassion. Attributes an actor carries with them for life.

PAUL ROSEBY, CEO AND ARTISTIC DIRECTOR OF THE NATIONAL
YOUTH THEATRE

INTRODUCTION

One of the most magical moments when teaching acting is when a student lets go of all inhibitions and gives a truthful performance. It's in this book I provide exercises that will hopefully bring many of these moments.

I've been lucky to teach in wide variety of settings. I've taught acting at youth theatres, after-school clubs, part-time theatre schools, state schools, special needs schools, private schools and a centre for teenagers who have been expelled. These students all had one thing in common – they wanted to be up on their feet putting learning into practice. Therefore, this is a highly practical book.

Over the 12 years I taught acting, I created and developed a wide range of exercises to help students improve their acting technique. As an acting teacher I wanted to help students reach their goals. Students often had goals such as getting into drama school, becoming a professional actor or improving grades at school for a practical exam. I'm proud that many of my students were successful at achieving their goals. Although the activities in this book will help the budding actor, they also help in other areas of development too, including confidence, creativity, understanding of oneself and others, social skills, team work skills and imagination.

Many students would start their time with me with a shield on, either trying to be the funniest, smartest, loudest or most shy. But slowly I would de-shield these students and underneath find something far more exciting – their true selves! Once students stopped trying to be something they're not and were comfortable with being who they truly are, that's when the magic began. Many of the exercises at the beginning of this book help to break down some of the protective habits students might have formed. Other exercises later on in the book focus on improvisation skills and on working with text.

Some of the activities in this book were inspired by classical practitioners such as Konstantin Stanislavsky, Uta Hagen, Lee Strasberg and Sanford Meisner. The techniques these practitioners created are still used today on film and TV sets, by drama schools, and in professional theatre rehearsals. Some of the exercises in this book are very similar to these original exercises by these classical practitioners, and others have been adapted, so they are safe and fun for younger students. Other exercises have been entirely created by me and are the ones I found to work best in the classroom.

All of the exercises in his book aim to unleash inner creativity, to expand imaginations and to bring truth and feeling to a performance. The exercises can be used for drama workshops and acting lessons. They can also be used to help students prepare for practical exams, auditions and shows. Although this book is mainly aimed at drama and English teachers, it can also be used by drama students as many of the exercises can be practised alone at home.

My hope is that the exercises in this book will inspire young people to be true to themselves and to perform from a place of truth.

Method acting and safety

Although some of the exercises in this book are linked to method acting, no affective memory or emotional recall practices are included. These techniques should not be attempted until the student is over the age of 18 and with an experienced practitioner. Affective memory exercises are central to method acting and require the actor to recall memories (often emotional ones) and then apply these feelings to the character they are playing. I do not recommend that under-18s do this as it can bring to the surface all kinds of distressing traumas. Some argue that they shouldn't be practised at all.

However, I have included some lighter method acting techniques in this book. There are warnings next to these exercises as some teachers may not feel their class is ready for them, or they may not feel comfortable teaching them. The facilitator needs to tread carefully, remaining vigilant and aware of how the students are responding. The activity should be stopped immediately if someone is becoming distressed, and the teacher should make time to speak to the student who has become upset at the end of the class. In all the years I've taught, none of my students have become distressed during any of the exercises I've included in this book, but there is always the possibility.

Creating a safe space

My teaching philosophy is to create a safe space where students can fully be their creative selves. For me a safe space is an environment where students know they will be accepted for who they are and that they can talk about their feelings without fear of judgement. If students feel safe in the class, they will be able to improvise, perform and be creative. Students should never be afraid of failing, looking stupid or not being liked. Mistakes should be encouraged – celebrated even! Here are some tips for creating a safe space for students:

- Lay down the rules. Kindness and good listening are always my top two.

- Give constant positive feedback, and when giving constructive feedback, make sure to bring up the strong points as well as the weaker ones.

- Never tolerate bullying or any negative remarks or gestures in the classroom.

- Be patient. If you need to explain your drama activity a few times before the class understands, that's okay. Don't be hard on them.

- Never force a student to do any activity, and be clear that they are allowed to sit out and watch at any point during the class.

- Don't overcomplicate the lesson, and take small steps while facilitating an exercise so that everyone fully understands what they are doing.

- Encourage play and failure.

- Ask students to leave their inner critics outside the rehearsal place.

- Never allow students to talk over someone else's performance, and encourage them to clap and find positive things to say after someone has performed in front of the class.

- Ensure good discipline in the classroom. Do not tolerate any disruptive behaviour, and have a clear signal for silence.

Of course creating a *physically* safe space is important too. The teacher should always get to the classroom at least 10 minutes early and check for dangers such as stacked chairs, blocked fire exists, sharp objects on the floor and so on.

How to use this book

This book is designed as a dip in and out of resource book. It's a resource both for those who teach drama and for those who want to practise acting on their own. The material is suitable for English lessons, drama workshops, acting lessons, or for use when working towards a show, audition or exam piece and for private practical study at home.

This book is split into eleven chapters, each with its own introduction and a variety of exercises. The exercises at the start of each chapter are aimed at beginner/ younger students, and as each chapter progresses, the exercises get harder. Every chapter finishes with the more advanced exercises. Although the exercises in this book have been numbered, they can be taught in any order. However, I would advise that, before practising the more advanced material, one or two of the warm-up exercises be practised first.

Many teachers, in particular English, primary, elementary and middle school teachers, are asked to teach drama, even if they have never studied or taught the subject before. If this is you and you are reading this book, please don't panic! You don't need to have a degree or to have studied drama at college to teach it. However, you may need help, which hopefully this book can offer you. My hope is that this book will be a valuable resource to both the experienced and the inexperienced drama teachers. For those of you with less experience, choose the simpler exercises in this book and the ones you feel most comfortable with. Then, as your confidence as a drama teacher grows, you can build up to the more advanced exercises.

It is not recommended that the teacher create a lesson from only one chapter. For a well-balanced lesson, the teacher should take exercises from at least three or four different chapters. A well-balanced lesson might include one exercise from Chapter 1, 'Relaxation and Focus', one exercise from Chapter 2, 'Voice', one exercise from Chapter 3, 'Movement', one exercise from Chapter 4, 'Unblocking Performers' and two exercises from Chapter 6, 'Objectives'. For a lesson that is an hour in length, you should be using about four to seven exercises. Younger students may need more exercises in their lessons than older students so as to keep them engaged.

If you are an actor using this book on your own, be sure to practise only the exercises you are comfortable with and to warm up appropriately (the relaxation chapter is a good place to find a warm-up activity). Some of the exercises in this book can only be practised as a group, but there are many that can be practised alone. If you have an audition coming up, there are many exercises here that will hopefully help you improve your audition and acting technique. The actor and theatre practitioner Konstantin Stanislavsky did much of his learning alone at home, and I recommend that any budding actor do the same.

1 RELAXATION AND FOCUS

Introduction

Tension is one of the actor's greatest enemies, and most professional actors spend a lot of time practising relaxation exercises in the hope of obtaining a free and open body. Watching a tense actor can feel uncomfortable and false, and audiences are able to pick up on even the smallest of tensions. Therefore, relaxation work is a very important element to the actors training.

Life throws problems at all of us, and over the years, this baggage can show up in our bodies and voice. In general, actors between the ages of 8 and 11 don't hold very many tensions, and adult actors strive for this carefree childhood state of being. But sadly, from about the age of 11, tensions in the body start creeping in, and between the ages of 13 and 17, they can be particularly strong. Teenage actors have to work hard at relaxing their bodies so that they can be affective at their craft.

As soon as the actor walks into an audition, before they have even begun their audition material, the panel are usually looking to see what tensions the actor is carrying. Audition panels will instantly warm to an actor who has few tensions as they know this is likely to be someone flexible whom they can work with. A lot of training in acting is about teaching the student to be free and childlike again. The actor should practise relaxation techniques daily and strive for freedom and flexibility in the voice, body and mind. The exercises in this chapter will help with this.

While practising relaxation, it's important to remember that there is a difference between being sleepy and relaxed and being focused and relaxed. The actor is aiming for the latter, which is why I've titled this chapter 'Relaxation and Focus', rather than just 'Relaxation'. It is possible to be relaxed in a bad way: too laid back, sleepy or not fully present is not desirable. The actor needs to be tension-free, fully present and fully alert at the same time; think Yoda from *Star Wars*. Many meditation practices rooted in mindfulness teach practical ways of achieving this, which is why I've included a meditation teaching in this chapter.

1.1 Releasing tension while lying down

A simple relaxation exercise in which students relax each body part, one body part at a time, while lying down.

Age: 8 plus.
Skills: Concentration, awareness, focus, relaxation and mindfulness.
Participants: This exercise can be done alone or in a group.
Time: 10–40 minutes (depending on the age group).
You'll need: A warm room with a comfortable floor for students to lie on. If the room is cold, students should wear coats and/or use blankets to keep warm. If the floor is hard, students should lie on yoga mats or blankets.
How to: Ask the students to lie on the floor with their eyes closed. If the actor starts to feel sleepy during this exercise, they should open their eyes and try to bring the energy back into the body without moving; if they really need to, they can wiggle their toes or fingers to try and wake up.

Students need to try and bring their energy inwards, reclaiming it from others and different spaces, bringing their circle of attention in. Ask the students to notice the breath: is it slow, fast, steady, scattered? Is the breath in the chest, stomach or pelvic area? If it's up in the chest, or even the throat, bring the breath down so that it's lower in the body. The stomach, not the chest, should move up and down with each in- and out-breath.

Once the breath is stable, the actor can start relaxing each part of the body, one part at a time. They can start with softening the muscles in the forehead and then the eyebrows, the eyelids, the temples, the cheeks, the lips, the jaw, the tongue and any other parts of the face. It is important to spend a long time on the face as it's one of the main areas people hold tension. Once the actor has relaxed every part of the face, they can make very gentle 'blah blah' sounds, being careful to keep the tongue relaxed, as well as the face, as the sound is released.

Once the actor has finished relaxing the face, they can move onto the body. Ask the students to start with the neck, allowing it to sink into the floor. Then they should drop the shoulders, noticing where the shoulders are in contact with the floor. Ask students to try and increase the contact with the floor by loosening into the ground: imagine the upper part of the body is melting into the floor. Next ask students to bring the attention to the hands, letting the fingers, thumbs, palms and wrists melt into the ground. Talk then through working the attention up into the arms, releasing the tension from the forearm, elbow and upper arm. Now ask them to work the attention down the body, releasing the mid back and lower back, relaxing the abdominal muscles and then moving onto the lower body.

Explain that people vary – some tend to carry most of their tension in the lower body, others in the upper body and others in isolated areas such as the eyelids or jaw. Ask students to reflect on where they hold their tension. For the relaxation of the lower body, the actor can start by wiggling their toes and then relax the toes, the feet, the calf muscles, quad muscles, hamstrings, pelvis and buttocks.

Once every part of the body has been relaxed, ask the actor to imagine energy flowing in through the feet, up the legs, through the hips, up into the upper body and face. Allow this energy to move freely through the body with no blockages of tension. Allow a good few minutes for this sensation to arise, and when it is time to stand up, make sure the students really take their time; firstly you don't want them to get dizzy. But secondly it's important to keep the relaxation that was just achieved in the body while standing up.

Variation: It's also possible to do this exercise standing up with the back against a wall, or standing with no support or sitting down. If practising this exercise standing up, it's important to keep the feet hip-width apart.

Tip: Students shouldn't rush this exercise but take their time as they relax every part of the body. Anxieties and thoughts should be left outside of the rehearsal space.

The aim: For the actor to become more aware of their body and face, exploring where it is they are prone to holding tension and then releasing this.

1.2 A seated relaxation exercise

An exercise created by and taught by Lee Strasberg for releasing tension in the body and face.

Age: 8 plus.
Skills: Concentration, awareness, focus, relaxation and mindfulness.
Participants: This exercise can be done alone or in a group.
Time: 10–40 minutes (depending on the age group).
You'll need: A chair for every participant.
How to: This exercise should not be rushed, and students should be very thorough while practising it.

Ask students to sit on a straight-backed armless chair in a slumped position, a position in which they might be able to fall sleep. After getting into this comfortable position, the actor is ready to explore their body for tension.

Ask students to raise their right hand and investigate their fingers and hand for tension. They can move the hand and fingers around, scrunching their fingers slowly, circling their wrist or holding their hand still. The most important thing the student needs to ask is, **'Where is the tension?'** Once they have found it, they must willingly release it by asking the muscle to let go. Students should ask in their head, not out load.

Once the tension has been released in the hand, move onto the other hand. Talk students through every part of the body, taking time with each arm, shoulder, neck, stomach and so on. The actor can lift body parts and drop them down, circle them, tense them up and release. While doing the lips, for example, they can be fully stretched open, then spread out wide and scrunched up. For the exercise, everything must be done slowly, one body part at a time, but the most important thing is that the student keeps asking the same question, '**Where is the tension?**' Then once the tension is found, the student asks that tension to let go.

The student should spend a particularly long time on the face, paying attention to the cheeks, lips, temples, brow, eyelids, tongue and nose. The face is often where many mental tensions are held; the face is also one of the actor's most important tools, particularly for the film actor. Spend time around the throat area as a relaxed throat will help with voice work. If the actor feels tension in the throat, they can release this with a long sustained 'ahhhhh' sound or a staccato 'hah'. While exploring different areas, explain to the actor to be careful that tension doesn't go back into the areas that have already been relaxed.

Sometimes a student can have a strong emotional response while doing this exercise. If this happens, the student can either stop the exercise or continue.

Variation: Again the actor sits on a straight-backed armless chair in a slumped-down position, a position in which they might be able to sleep. The student closes their eyes, stays motionless and imagines that they are lying in the sun. The actor should try and remember what the sun feels like on their face. Get specific: does it feel hotter on the lips or eyelids than it does on the chin? How does it feel on the nose? How hot does the body feel? Is this mild or very strong sun beams? How different do the rays feel when they hit a clothed area as opposed to an area of bare skin? Become aware of how the heat may have relaxed the muscles. Now, one body part at a time, focus on the sun beams releasing the tension there while keeping still. Start with the face; imagine the sun beams releasing all the tension there, melting it away. Then move onto the neck, the chest, the shoulders and so on.

Tip: Students should be encouraged to have an open mind while practising this exercise and understand that a lot of tension in the body is created by the mind, so it is also the mind that has the power to release the tension.

The aim: The aim of this exercise is for the actor to identify where the tension in the body is and then to actively release it with the mind. After practising this exercise for some months, or maybe weeks, the hope is that students will learn how to identify and expel unwanted tension quickly.

1.3 Awareness of energy

A warm-up to heighten awareness where students will walk around the room at a very slow pace.

Age: 8 plus.
Skills: Concentration, awareness, focus, relaxation and movement.

Participants: This exercise can be done alone or in a group.

Time: 10–15 minutes.

You'll need: A quiet space for participants to move around in.

How to: Ask the group to stand in a circle or, if practising on your own, stand in a space in the room. The student stands with the feet hip-width apart and the spine in a neutral position, letting the arms relax by the sides of the body. The weight on both feet should be distributed evenly with not too much weight on the balls, heels or sides of the feet. Now ask the students to notice their breath; is it shallow or deep, and where is it coming from? The actor should then take a deep breath in from the stomach and, while breathing in, lengthen the spine.

Now ask students to breath out, and as they breathe out, they create space within themselves. Do three or four long breaths with these instructions.

Next instruct students through a spinal roll. For this, the student stands up tall and then tucks in their chin, lengthening the back of the neck. Let the shoulders drop down, bend the bottom of the back and bend the knees slightly and fold the body over itself, so the arms are dangling down loose with the finger tips or hands touching the floor. Instruct the students to keep the head, shoulders and neck relaxed and floppy. Keeping the body draped forward and tucking the pelvis in, ask participants to take a long breath in and then out. Now the students can slowly roll back up through the spine, one vertebra at a time. This should not be rushed, and the neck should be the last part of the body that is lifted into the standing position.

When the students are standing tall and relaxed, the teacher can ask some questions. Ask students to notice where their centre of energy is – the stomach, face, hips, eyes, lips or hands? Ask them to become aware of where they hold their energy and encourage them to spread it more evenly throughout the body. Ask them to imagine energy coming up from the ground, into their feet, up through both legs and into the whole of their body. Ask them to notice if there are any blockages, and if there are, can they try and release them?

Now ask students to take one step very slowly, completely aware of how the foot makes contact with the floor. Ask which part of the foot moves first. When does the foot lift? Which part of the foot is the last part to make contact with the ground before it lifts up into a step? Ask the students to very slowly walk around the room, instructing them to be aware and conscious of every movement in the body, from the bending of the knee to the movement in the back. Ask them to be aware of how the centre of energy in the body may change as they move, and encourage them to allow that energy to move freely through the body.

Variation one: It's also possible to practise part of this exercise by either lying down or sitting on a chair. If this version is practised, the teacher can ask the student about how their spine feels against the floor or back of the chair.

Variation two: This exercise can be done with the eyes closed. By eliminating the sight, it can make the participants hyper-aware of their bodies and movements, especially while practising the part of the exercises where students slowly walk around the room. If this activity is practised with the eyes closed, make sure there are no hazards in the room such as staked chairs or things on the floor to trip on, and ask students to walk very slowly and to only take two or three steps during the walking part of the activity. The teacher will need to watch all students very carefully as they walk and call *Stop* if they see an accident approaching.

Tip: Being aware of the breath is very important while practising exercises that promote awareness, so during the exercise, keep reminding to students to notice their breath.

The aim: For the actor to become highly aware of their body and movements.

1.4 Counting to twenty

A group activity where students work together to count to twenty.

Age: 8 plus.

Skills: Concentration, awareness, focus, movement, patience, listening and mindfulness.

Participants: This exercise needs to be practised in groups of five or more.

Time: 5–10 minutes.

You'll need: A space for students where they can lie quietly on the floor with their eyes closed.

How to: Students find a space in the room, lie down on the floor and close their eyes. Ask them to listen to all of the noises they can hear around them and to focus on these sounds. Ask them to listen to any noises they can hear in the room and outside of the room. After a few minutes of listening, the teacher can introduce the exercises.

The group is going to count from one to twenty, with each number said by one person. If two people say a number at the same time, the group starts again from number one. It's important that students don't look at each other during this activity.

Variations: The experienced group can try for a higher number to count up to fifty or perhaps even 100. It's also possible to do this activity counting backwards, down from twenty to one. Or if the group is working on a group poem or chorus piece in class, the group can say the piece, one word at a time, one person at a time. If two people say a word at the same time, the group starts again from the beginning of the piece.

Tip: Encourage students to remain patient and forgiving of one another every time the group has to start at number one again.

The aim: To encourage the group to focus on one another, work as a team, stay patient and really listen.

1.5 Meditation

A practice to enable the actor to become more mindful.

Age: 8 plus.
Skills: Concentration, awareness, focus, mindfulness and charisma.
Participants: This exercise can be done alone or in a group.
Time: 10–30 minutes.
You'll need: A quiet space and a cushion for each student. A meditation cushion is ideal; however, any cushion or pillow will be adequate.
How to: There are many different ways to meditate, but here's a simple breathing practice to get the students started.

Students find a space in the room and sit on their cushion or pillow, cross-legged with their knees in contact with the floor. Students can sit on the cushion either cross-legged or in half lotus or full lotus posture. If the student would prefer to sit on a chair, that is possible too. Whether the student is sitting on a cushion or chair, they need to sit up straight, holding their own spine up without leaning on anything. Once seated, the teacher can ask the students to notice what parts of their body are in contact with the ground, cushion or chair. If on a chair, both of the feet should be planted on the ground, and if on a cushion, the knees should be in contact with the floor. If the knees don't reach the ground, it's possible to use cushions or clothing for support.

Now ask the students to focus on the breath. Ask them to notice each in- and out-breath without forcing or changing anything. After a few moments of this, ask them to breathe deep and slow. The teacher can say several times, 'I breathe in I breathe deep. I breathe out I breathe slow.' After a few minutes of this, explain that during meditations, feelings can arise. Reassure students that these feelings are normal and they should accept them; there's no need to fight feelings. Allow the feelings to arise and pass at their own will. Explain that they should let the feeling come, let it stay and then let it pass; accept thoughts and feelings with a loving eye and continue to focus on the breathing. Breathing in, and breathing out. Allow students to sit for 5–10 minutes in silence as they focus on their breathing. If the legs or feet start to hurt during the meditation it is okay to gently adjust the position.

Now ask the students to count the breath. When the student breathes in, they count one in their head, and when they breathe out, they count one again. Then two on the in-breath and two on the out-breath. They continue this with slow deep breaths until they get to ten. If they lose count, they can start again from number one. This exercise helps the beginner let go of thoughts and focus on the breath.

Variation: Another meditation involves becoming aware of each body part. The teacher can start with a few minutes of quiet breathing and then ask the students to focus on each body part, one body part at a time. The teacher may start at the toes, asking the students to become aware of each toe, the gap between the toes and tensions in the toes. Then the teacher should encourage the student to be grateful for their toes. Part of meditation practice is to learn to accept, become aware of and be grateful for our bodies. The teacher moves through all the body parts in the same way described for the toes.

Tip: Many notable actors meditate as it is the ultimate way to become aware of the body and mind, to become more present and to arrive fully into the moment. To really feel the full benefits of meditation, the student should practise for 20–40 minutes a day for some months.

The aim: The aim is for the student to become fully mindful of the breath and the body and to be present in the moment without distraction.

1.6 Circles of attention

A group warm-up based on the concept of 'circles of attention', as taught by Konstantin Stanislavsky.

Age: 8 plus.
Skills: Concentration, awareness, focus, group awareness and charisma.
Participants: This is a group exercise.
Time: 10–15 minutes.
You'll need: A quiet space for participants to lie down and move around in.
How to: There are three circles of attention. Stanislavsky refers to the first circle of attention as 'solitude in public'. This is the smallest circle of attention where the actor focuses their attention inwards on themselves or on an object they are holding or which is very close by.

In the second circle of attention, the actor focuses their attention on themselves and the character they are interacting with or a nearby object in the room.

In the third circle of attention, the actor will have a more scattered demeanour as they allow the focus to spread across the whole room or set.

A good way for the teacher to introduce this practice to students is to ask them to lie down in a quiet space and focus on a small circle of attention. Ask students to imagine there is a small circle around them and to keep their attention contained to this circle; this is 'solitude in public' put into practice. The actor can focus on their hands, feet or the whole body so long as this state of attention is inward looking and contained. If the attention starts to move outside of this circle, the student can gently encourage it back in. For this small circle of attention, another possibility is to ask the students to imagine they are holding an object and then ask them to direct their attention to that object.

After about 5 minutes of 'solitude in public', ask the students to slowly move onto the second state of attention. This is a larger circle, extending about as far as someone who is talking distance away. Ask the students to stand up and spread their attention to someone nearby; they can greet that person, say hello and ask how they are. Or, if they'd prefer, they can direct their attention to a nearby object.

After a short time of practising the second circle of attention, students can move onto the third circle of attention; this is where they are interested in everything in the room. They may notice many different people and objects as they walk around, and they may notice that their attention feels much more scattered.

Variation one: Ask the students to walk around the room in the first circle of attention, reminding them not to pay attention to anyone or anything around them. Ask the students to think of a reason why they are walking around in this small circle of attention. Perhaps they are very shy and it's their first day at a new school, or they have just lost their beloved pet hamster and they don't want to tell anyone, or they are a day dreamer and they are thinking up a brand-new exciting story!

After a few minutes, tell the students that they will now walk around the room in the second circle of attention. Ask the students to find one person in the room and focus their attention on that person. Perhaps this person is a celebrity they admire, or an enemy at school, or a person they are keen to make friends with. Now have the group walk around the room like this, but explain that students can only focus their attention on someone who hasn't chosen them; otherwise the two participants will just stand staring at each other.

Now ask the students to walk around the room in the third circle of attention. The students' attention can now be scattered across the room; they may be interested in different people and objects around the room. Perhaps they are in a new school, interested in everything around them, or they are looking for something they have lost, or they have walked through a wardrobe and they are in a new and magical world.

Variation two: Students can apply circles of attention to a scene to put this teaching into practice. Ask students to get into pairs, hand out a short duologue and give them 10 to 15 minutes to rehearse this duologue. The actors should choose a circle of attention that suits the character in the scene. If students were given the below script, it would work for Sara to play a large circle of attention and for Becky to play a small one. For the boys in the class, explain that Becky can be changed into a male character called Bernard!

A Little Princess

Written by Frances Hodgson Burnett, adapted by Samantha Marsden.

Cast: Sara and Becky

Becky is a child servant cleaning Sara's bedroom. Sara is a very rich child, living in a boarding school. Becky has finished cleaning Sara's room and has fallen asleep in Sara's armchair.

lks in and Becky wakes up startled.

Oh miss. I'm sorry Miss.

It's okay. It doesn't matter.

Becky   I didn't mean to fall asleep, it was the warm fire and I was so tired, I shouldn't have sat in your chair. I'm so sorry Miss ….

Sara   It's okay. You were tired, you couldn't help it.

Becky   Ain't you angry, miss? Ain't you going to tell on me?

Sara   No! Of course I'm not! Why, we are just the same – I am only a little girl like you. It's just an accident that I am not you, and you are not me.

Becky (*confused*)   An accident?

Sara   Yes. Have you done your work? Dare you stay a few minutes?

Becky   Here, miss? Me?

Sara checks no one is in the hallway.

Sara   No one is anywhere about. If you've finished cleaning all the bedrooms perhaps you might stay a tiny while in mine? I thought perhaps you might like a piece of cake.

Sara gets Becky a piece of cake, Becky eats it fast.

Sara   You're hungry?

Becky nods. Sara hands her another piece of cake.

Sara   Here's some for later too.

Becky   Thank you miss.

Sara   Please don't call me miss, call me Sara.

Becky nods.

Becky (*pointing to a dress hanging up*)   Is that your best dress?

Sara   It's one of my dancing dresses, I like it. Don't you?

Becky   Very much miss. It's like one a princess would wear.

Sara   I've often thought that I should like to be princess; I wonder what it feels like. I think from now on I will pretend to be one.

Variation three: It can also be fun to add circles of attention to an improvisation too. Ask students to get into pairs. Explain that they are going to create a 5-minute improvisation. In this improvisation, each character must have one want, and this want can be anything: to go to Brazil, to get a puppy or to design a flying car. Once each actor has thought up an objective, ask them to add a circle of attention to that character. Ideally the pair should choose characters with different circles of attention so as to create humour and/or conflict within the scene. Give the students about 5 minutes to practise the improvisation and then ask them to show the improvisation to the rest of the class. The audience can then try to guess which circles of attention each actor was playing.

Tip: Remember this exercise is an internal one and not a show. Students should avoid acting out the circles of attention and instead focus on noticing them.

The aim: The aim of circles of attention is to draw the actor's attention away from the audience and into the story they are performing. Circles of attention is a great tool to help improve the focus and charisma of any performance. One challenge the actor faces is that they must give the illusion that they are being private, even though they are in a public space; this exercise helps with this.

2 VOICE

Introduction

The foundation of all voice work is relaxation and breathing. Young children breathe correctly with no obstructions, and it's as we get older that we forget how to breathe. Actors work at returning to the vocal freedom they were born with. Baby and toddler voices can be loud, expressive and open, especially when crying. The infant rarely experiences any of the blocks or tensions that can be heard in the voices of older children, teenagers and adults. Relaxation work, especially for students aged 11 plus, is particularly important when working on the voice. If tensions show up in the throat or chest, the actor will struggle to deliver their lines in an expressive way. Every acting class, even for children, should begin with some basic breathing and relaxation exercises. Some of the exercises in this chapter can be used to reinforce work done in Chapter 1, 'Relaxation and Focus'.

Everybody is born with a highly versatile voice capable of a wide range of sounds and notes. But from a very young age, children start to suppress their vocal abilities. Adults are often telling children to use their quiet voice, not to scream, or to calm down, and sadly vocal abilities get dulled. The main problem I have when teaching children and teenagers is getting them to project; very often they are too scared to let go and make a noise loud enough for the whole of the auditorium to hear. In this chapter I provide some exercises to help students relax, let go, project and explore their voices in a fun and positive way.

2.1 Relaxation and breathing exercise

A relaxation and breathing exercise where students relax each part of their vocal apparatus and learn to breathe deeply.

Age: 8 plus.
Skills: Concentration, awareness, focus, relaxation, breathing and voice.
Participants: This exercise can be done alone or in a group.

Time: 10–30 minutes (depending on the age group).

You'll need: A warm room with a comfortable floor for students to lie on. If the room is cold, students should wear coats and/or use blankets to keep warm. If the floor is hard, students should lie on yoga mats or blankets. For the diaphragm work, students will need a lightweight object such as a small paperback book.

How to (relaxation): Ask the students to lie down and let any of the stresses of the day leave the room. Explain to them that the key to unlocking the voice's potential is being able to relax the instrument and free it of any stresses and inhibitions. Ask them to close their eyes. Now spend a few minutes asking them to relax parts of the face and body, one part at a time, including the forehead, temples, eyelids, cheeks, lips, neck, inside of the throat, shoulders, chest and torso. Ask the students if their eyelids are flickering or if they are tightly closed; if they are, ask them to try and relax the mind and to let their thoughts go. Tense eyelids are often a sign of a busy mind.

Once the face is relaxed, ask the students to relax the jaw. Ask them to use both hands to gently move the jaw up and down. This must be done very gently and the jaw should never be moved from side to side. It should be a relaxed, calm, up-and-down movement. After moving the jaw up and down for a few minutes, ask the students to put their hands by their sides and to relax their tongues. After a few moments, they can make 'la, la, la' noises as if they have just been to the dentist and had an anaesthetic. The jaw, face and tongue should all be very floppy. Keeping this floppy state, change the sounds from 'la, la, la' to 'blah, blah, blah' to 'fa, fa, fa' to 'as, as, as'. A whole variety of sounds work for this so long as they are short sounds and they can be repeated. Reassure students that it doesn't matter what they look or sound like during this, and if they dribble, who cares!

Now ask the students to notice where their breath is. Is it high in the chest? Low in the chest? Or in the stomach? If the breath is in the upper torso, this may mean there is some tension there which needs releasing. Students should aim to bring their breath into their stomachs.

How to (diaphragm work): One of the keys to correct breathing is to use the diaphragm. The diaphragm is a large muscle just underneath the ribcage. Ask the students to lie down on the floor, backs flat, arms by the side and knees bent so that their knees are pointing up to the ceiling. Now the student can either put their hands on their diaphragm or put a lightweight object on it. A lightweight paperback book is a good option. Students can now watch to see how this object moves as they breathe. It should move upwards with the in-breath and downwards with the out-breath. Some students, particularly older ones, may find that the opposite is true, with their diaphragm moving downwards as they breathe in and up as they breathe out. If this is the case, ask the students to correct it, explaining that their diaphragm needs to go up as they breathe in and down as they breathe out.

Some students may notice that their object doesn't move at all; this may be because they are not breathing deeply enough. Perhaps they are breathing from their chests. Ask them to relax their upper bodies and to bring the breath down into the diaphragm. Practise this regularly with the aim of everyone in the class getting the object to move in the right direction with the breath.

Now the students are ready to add voice to the out-breath. Ask them to take a deep breath in, raising the diaphragm, then with the out-breath, they can use the voice to let out an 'aaaaaa' with the breath. This 'aaaaaa' should come from the diaphragm. Repeat this for all the vowels: *a, e, i, o* and *u*.

The next stage of this exercise is to practise correct breathing and releasing a sound with the breath while standing up (this time using hands and not an object to check the diaphragm). Then the next stage after standing is to practise walking around the room with the correct breath, and after that, jogging!

Tip: Explain to students that they should never feel embarrassed or ashamed of their voice and it's okay to make bizarre sounds with it in the drama class.

The aim: To relax the vocal apparatus, teaching students how to engage their diaphragms and to connect the voice with the breath.

2.2 Diction and tongue-twisters

Vocal exercises to help students with speech and projection.

Age: 8 plus.
Skills: Voice, diction, speech and projection.
Participants: This exercise can be done alone or in a group.
Time: 5–15 minutes.
You'll need: A space for students to stand in a circle.
How to: Ask students to stand in a circle and to check their posture. The feet should be hip-width apart and the spine pulled up gently from the tip of the head. Start the warm-up by asking the students to open their mouths really wide and then quickly scrunch their lips up into a really tight prune shape. Repeat opening and closing the mouth like this three or four times. Now ask the students to place their hands on their diaphragms. With the in-breath the diaphragm pushes out the hand and with the out-breath the diaphragm contracts. Ask the students to think of their diaphragm as a balloon: with the in-breath the balloon blows up, filling with air, and with the out-breath the air is released, making the balloon shrink. After a few of these deep breaths in and out, ask the students to make a humming sound on the out-breath. Breathe in together to the count of three, expanding the diaphragm, and breathe out on a hum to the count of six. Explain to the students that they should choose one note and that sound should come from deep down in the pelvic area. This humming noise should vibrate the torso and lips; if it's not doing so, ask the students to hum a little louder and deeper.

Now explain to the students that diction is very important, particularly in theatre work. Good diction will help the audience to hear and understand the actor. I find that diction is particularly a problem with younger students. For good diction, explain that consonants need to be pronounced very clearly at the beginning and end of each word. The 21 consonant letters in the English alphabet are b, c, d, f, g, h, j, k, l, m, n, p, q, r, s, t, v, x, z and usually w and y. Say a consonant, for example, 'b, b, b, b', and then ask the students to say it with you, 'b, b, b, b'. Do this for at least five or six constants, or go through all of them if the class is older and focused. Now do the same for some constant sounds such as ch, sh and th. Now move onto some words that start and end in a consonant, asking students to really emphasize pronouncing the letters. Some examples include bed, sack, hat, tall, Bob, fizz, frozen and Jack.

After this group warm-up, give the group some tongue-twisters to work on; these can be said as a group altogether or in smaller groups. Once the group knows each other well, you can ask students to say a tongue-twister on their own in front of the group; however, they must never be forced to do this.

Tongue-twisters

Red lorry, yellow lorry.
Red lorry, yellow lorry.
Red lorry, yellow lorry.
Red lorry, yellow lorry.

...

She sells sea shells on the sea shore.
She sells sea shells on the sea shore.
She sells sea shells on the sea shore.
She sells sea shells on the sea shore.

...

Round and round the rugged rock the ragged rascal ran.
Round and round the rugged rock the ragged rascal ran.
Round and round the rugged rock the ragged rascal ran.
Round and round the rugged rock the ragged rascal ran.

...

I scream, you scream, we all scream for ice cream.
I scream, you scream, we all scream for ice cream.
I scream, you scream, we all scream for ice cream.
I scream, you scream, we all scream for ice cream.

...

Toy boat.
Toy boat.
Toy boat.
Toy boat.

…

A proper copper coffee pot.
A proper copper coffee pot.
A proper copper coffee pot.
A proper copper coffee pot.

…

Unique New York.
Unique New York.
Unique New York.
Unique New York.

…

A big black bear ate a big black bug.
A big black bear ate a big black bug.
A big black bear ate a big black bug.
A big black bear ate a big black bug.

…

Eleven benevolent elephants.
Eleven benevolent elephants.
Eleven benevolent elephants.
Eleven benevolent elephants.

Variation: You can ask the students to invent some of their own tongue-twisters.

Tip: Listen and learn from news readers, theatre actors, good public speakers (and fingers-crossed drama teachers!) to hear how they use their voices to communicate clearly.

The aim: To help students to speak with good diction.

2.3 Pass the vowel

A fun fast-paced game to warm up and liberate the voice.

Age: 8 plus.
Skills: Voice, diction, speech, fast thinking, listening, energy and projection.

Participants: For a group of five or more.

Time: 5–10 minutes.

You'll need: A space for students to stand in a circle.

How to: Ask the students to stand in a circle and remind them of the five vowels: *a, e, i, o* and *u*. Explain that each time they say a vowel, it will be extended, almost slightly sung, for example, 'aaaaaa'. It can be a good idea to get the whole class to make the noise of each vowel altogether first so as to break the ice.

One person will start the game off by miming the action of throwing a ball to someone else in the circle while saying/singing the vowel. This person might, for example, say 'eeeeee' as they throw the imaginary ball to someone else standing in the circle. The person whom the 'eeeeee' was thrown to mimes catching it and repeats the sound, 'eeeeee', and then without hesitation, they throw a different vowel to someone else in the circle, 'oooooooo'. If the person hesitates, says um, repeats the same vowel that was thrown at them, or says a sound that isn't a vowel, they are out and they sit down where they are standing in the circle. As the players diminish, the game should get faster and more competitive. It will finish with just two people throwing vowels at each other; these two players are the winners of the game.

Variation: A more advanced version of this game for older or well-practised students is to play it exactly the same way but to use words instead of sounds. But these words have to have vowels in the centre of them. The vowel is said in an extended almost sing-song way. For example, 'beeeeed', 'gloooooow', 'siiiiiiiiit' and 'faaaaaaaake'.

Tip: Do a group vocal warm-up before playing this game so that the students have been full warmed up vocally; this way they will feel less inhibited.

The aim: To encourage spontaneity, to release inhibitions and to open up the voice.

2.4 Pass the chewing gum

A fun warm-up game where students pass some imaginary chewing gum around the circle.

Age: 8 plus.

Skills: Imagination, confidence, group awareness and relaxation.

Participants: For a group of five or more.

Time: 5 minutes.

You'll need: A group of students to stand in a circle.

How to: Students stand in a circle and the teacher takes an imaginary piece of chewing gum from behind their own ear. The teacher explains that this is a magic piece of gum and it is constantly changing flavour. And in order to really get the most out of this chewing gum, the student has to chew hard. The teacher then pops the gum into their mouth and chews, making 'mmmm' noises and perhaps even communicating the flavour between chews, 'mmmm red velvet cake flavour!' Then after a melodramatic chewing session, the teacher passes it on to the next student who will take the imaginary gum and chew it. The gum gets passed around until everyone gets a chew.

Tip: Make it a really large imaginary piece of gum!

The aim: For students to loosen up their jaws in an imaginative and fun way.

2.5 Soundscape

A simple and creative game where players create scenes with sound.

Age: 8 plus.

Skills: Voice, imagination, energy and projection.

Participants: For a group of five or more.

Time: 5–10 minutes.

You'll need: A space for students to sit in a circle.

How to: Students sit in a circle, and the teacher explains that they are going to create the atmosphere of a place with sounds. Let's start with a fairground. Students can make any noise they like from the fairground; give them some examples and ideas to start with: pop corn popping, laughing, someone saying 'tickets please' or musical sounds. Ask someone to start: they must repeat their chosen noise, or the phrase, over and over again. Then the person next to that student adds their noise; then the person next to them adds their own noise and so on. If someone doesn't want to add a noise, they can shake their head to signal that they'd like to pass. For younger students, the teacher may need to point at the students when it's their turn to add a noise. Once everyone is doing their fairground noise, the teacher can lift their hands like a conductor to signal an increase in volume and bring their hands down to decrease the volume; this can be done several times. Then the teacher gestures their hands into the cut position and asks everyone for silence.

This can be repeated, but for the second round, it can be fun to ask if a student would like to sit in the centre of the circle and be the conductor instead of the teacher. Show this volunteer the action for increasing volume, decreasing it and silence. Most students will love having the power of being the conductor, and it can be good for those who need a little boost in confidence. Ask the students for the next idea for the soundscape. Ideas may include the seaside, school, London, New York, the jungle, Disney World, the zoo, a chocolate factory or fairy land. No idea should be dismissed, and the group should go with any suggestion.

Variation one: Ask the students to split into groups of five or six to create their own soundscapes. Give them 4 or 5 minutes to practise it as a team. Then have them perform these soundscapes to the rest of the group without saying what the soundscape is. The group should be able to guess the soundscape by listening.

Variation two: Split students into groups of six to eight. Half the group (three to four students) will make sound effects while the other half improvise a scene at a noisy location. For example, four students will sit down and watch the other four improvise a scene at the fair ground, and four sitting down will make appropriate fairground sound affects to enhance the scene.

Tip: This exercise can get load, so it's a good idea for the teacher to have a signal for silence. The signal might be when the teacher raises both hands into the air the class falls silent. Practise this signal with the class a few times before starting the game.

The aim: To encourage students to use their voices imaginatively.

2.6 Name game

A 'get to know each other' game where students introduce themselves with confidence. This is a particularly good game for younger students.

Age: 8 plus.
Skills: Voice, confidence, energy, trust, listening, spontaneity and projection.
Participants: For a group of five or more.
Time: 5–10 minutes.
You'll need: A space for students to stand in a circle.
How to: Ask the students to stand in a circle. One at a time each student will say their name, accompanied by an action. Then the rest of the group will copy this sound and action. The students may want to say their name short and staccato, 'Sam!', or in a long and low voice, 'Saaaaaaaaaam', or in a fluttery sing-song voice, 'SaAaAaAam'. Nothing is too wacky, but encourage the students to do this in a voice loud enough for everyone to hear. No action is too crazy either; students may want to jump, twirl or stamp as they say their name. The key to this game is that the whole group copies the action and sound of the student introducing themselves. This lets the performing student know that their voice, action and imagination have been accepted by the group. Go around the circle encouraging each student to contribute, but if someone doesn't want to say their name in front of the group, do not force them and allow them to just say pass. If you play this game for 2 or 3 weeks, by week 3 it is highly likely that every student will be keen to participate, even the most shy!

Theming: This game can be themed. Let's imagine that you are leading a fairy-tale workshop. In this case the game could be played as above, but instead of students saying their own name, they would say the name of a fairy-tale character and then they would perform the voice and an action for that character. For example, the student may step forward and introduce themselves as 'the big bad wolf, grrrrrrr!'; they may flare their lips and spread their hands out into claws. Then all the other students would repeat this sound and action.

Tip: Go round the circle and ask everyone to say their name once (in a normal way) to break the ice.

The aim: To give every student the confidence to speak up in front of a group.

2.7 Vocal forest

A warm-up game for releasing vocal tensions.

Age: 8 plus.
Skills: Voice, spontaneity, awareness and projection.
Participants: This can be done alone or in a group.
Time: 10–15 minutes.
You'll need: A space for students to stand spread out around the room.
How to: Ask the students to find a place in the room and take a position as a tree. Then when they are ready, they can let out any vocal expression they want. Maybe a short 'ha', or a long 'meeeeeee', or a quiet 'la'. It can be any sound so long as it's not actual words. With each noise, the aim is to release tension. Each time the student releases a noise, they move to a different tree pose and freeze. They then wait until the urge to release another vocal expression comes; they may wait a few seconds or minutes. When the urge comes, they release the sound and change position. Challenge the students not to plan the sound or new position and to act on impulse and feelings. Some students may make a sound and move every few seconds, others every few minutes. It's important to encourage students to follow their gut and not to mimic others.
Tip: Make sure the group has vocally warmed up so that they feel less inhibited.
The aim: To encourage students to connect to feelings through the voice and to release tensions.

2.8 Hello, my name is …

A very simple name game where students play with and warm up their voices. It's a particularly useful exercise for younger or shy students.

Age: 8 plus.
Skills: Voice, creativity, social skills, listening and projection.
Participants: For a group of five or more.
Time: 5–10 minutes.
You'll need: A space where students can sit in a circle.
How to: Ask the students sit in a circle on the floor or on chairs. One at a time each will say, 'Hello, my name is … ', filling the gap with their name, followed by 'I would like a … please', filling the gap with an vocal instruction. So the first student might say, 'Hello, my name is Aamir and I'd like a shout please.' The whole group would then shout, 'HELLO, AAMIR!'

Give students different options to choose from, for example, a shout, growl, squeak, song, whisper, murmur, bellow or any other sound. The game continues with everyone in the group having a turn, each choosing their own style of greeting.

Tip: For younger students only give three options – a shout, whisper or squeak. But for older students, give them free rein to use any description of a vocal sound that they'd like, for example, a song, growl, roar or blurt.

The aim: To make everyone in the group feel welcome and accepted. It also works as a vocal warm-up and a 'getting to know each other's name' game.

2.9 Good evening, Your Majesty

A fun warm-up game where students use their imaginations to disguise their voices.

Age: 8 plus.
Skills: Voice, imagination, listening and projection.
Participants: For a group of five or more.
Time: 5–10 minutes.
You'll need: The students have to know each other's names before playing this game. Any space is suitable for this exercise.
How to: One person, let's call her Keira, stands with her back to the group at one end of the room. The group stands at the other side of the room, standing really close to one another (shoulder to shoulder) in a huddle. The teacher asks someone in the group to silently volunteer. Let's say Iman volunteers. Iman will then disguise his voice and say 'Good evening, Your Majesty' to Keira. Keira has her back turned to the group and has to guess whom the voice belongs to. Iman's aim is for Keira not to guess it's him. Iman can do whatever he likes with his voice to disguise it; he may make it low or high, or speak slow or fast, or he may even try an accent. If Keira guesses wrong, she stays as the majesty with her back turned to the group; another person is chosen to say 'Good evening, Your Majesty' and Keira has to guess again. If Keira guesses the identity of the voice, she joins the group and someone else gets to have a turn at being the majesty.
Tip: Encourage students to project their voice and to speak from their stomach rather than from their throat.
The aim: To encourage students to play with their voices in a fun way.

2.10 Projection

An exercise to help students with projection.

Age: 8 plus.
Skills: Voice, confidence and projection.

Participants: This exercise can be done alone or in a group.

Time: 5 minutes to an hour.

You'll need: A large space outside.

How to: Very often a play is rehearsed in a classroom or studio, and then when it's transported from the rehearsal space to the stage, all the volume gets lost because in many cases the theatre is a bigger space than students are used to rehearsing in. This is particularly a problem with younger students. On show day, it's not uncommon to find the director at the back of the auditorium shouting down to the cast 'speak up' and 'I can't hear you!' But often it's too late as the show is on later that day and the cast are too used to rehearsing in a smaller space; thus, they are stuck at their low volume. It's particularly important with younger casts (under 13 years) to get them used to performing in different spaces. The voice sounds very different in different spaces, and students need to get used to this from as early on in the rehearsal process as possible. Personally, I like to take students outside two or three times during the rehearsal process as open air acoustics are the hardest. If you can get the cast to project well in an outside space, they'll cope with any auditorium. Outside there are no walls for the voice to bounce off, and sometimes there are distracting noises such as traffic, people and planes. Getting the cast used to distractions while performing is another bonus.

Before you ask students to project their voices, there are some things you should do first to ensure good vocal hygiene. These include:

- A thorough vocal warm-up. Explain to students that projecting their voices should never hurt, and if it hurts in any way, they must stop and tell the teacher.

- Make sure students know proper breathing techniques and encourage them to use these while on stage. The actor should breathe in using the diaphragm and speak on the out-breath.

- Explain to students that there's a big difference between shouting and projecting and that shouting can damage the vocal cords. Explain to students that when they are projecting from their diaphragm, their voices will sound deeper and fuller. Shouting and yelling will sound higher pitched and will make the throat sore.

- If a student is struggling to project, ask them to breathe in from the diaphragm and let out a loud 'ha' noise on the out-breath. Do a few of these and then try their line from the show.

- It is very important that students project from their stomachs, not from their chests or, even worse, from their throats. To project successfully students will need to bring their voices down low into the torso.

- If you are working on a play, take it outdoors and run the whole show outside, either with the actions (blocking) or without. The director should sit a good distance away from the cast, calling 'I can't hear' every time a cast member needs to project further. If you're not working on a play or text, the teacher can give students a short poem or phrase to work on outside.

Variation: Visualization can help some students to project their voices. The teacher can ask the students to make their voices hit a particular point, perhaps a tree or the auditorium wall. Challenge students to reach that point with their voice.

Tip: Challenge students with new spaces and distractions throughout the rehearsal process so that on the day of the show they are well prepared and don't lose their ability to project. During a final run-through, you can make your phone ring to teach the cast to speak up and carry on despite distractions!

The aim: To get students projecting their voices.

2.11 The song exercise

An advanced vocal exercise often used in method acting classes. The song exercise is used to release vocal tension and connect the actor's voice with emotion. This exercise must be practised with a group who knows each other well and is comfortable with each other.

Age: 13 plus.

Skills: Voice, trust and spontaneity.

Participants: Group of five or more.

Time: 30–60 minutes.

You'll need: A rehearsal room, and the students should have been in the class together and with their teacher for at least 6 months. The group dynamics have to be very positive and safe.

A note of caution: If a student wishes to stop this exercise at any point, it's very important that they are allowed to do so, and the teacher must make this very clear from the start of the exercise. This exercise can be so effective at releasing tension and connecting the voice to emotion that students can have a very emotional response. It's not uncommon for students to start laughing, or crying, or feeling angry while doing this exercise. If this happens, reassure students that an emotional response is normal and that the student should try and accept the feeling rather than fight it. Never put a student on the spot in front of the group by asking them to explain why they reacted in a certain way. Why an actor reacts emotionally to any situation is something the actor has the right to keep private. The teacher must never pry. However, of course, if the student wants to talk about it, let them know you are there for them to talk in private after class about anything.

How to: Before doing this exercise, it's good to do some relaxation and focus exercises from Chapter 1 first. Although there is singing involved in this exercise, this is not an exercise in singing. The student may be a beautiful singer or tone-deaf; either way it doesn't matter as this exercise is about freeing the voice of tensions, opening it up and connecting sound with emotion.

Instruct the class to sit in a long line along one side of the room and the student doing the singing exercise to stand on the other side of the room facing them. The actor now chooses a very simple and slow song that they know well. *Twinkle Twinkle Little Star* is a good choice if they can't think of another song. The actor now makes eye contact with the first person in the line opposite them. Then, when they are ready, they sing the first word from the song, 'twinkle', for example. They need to sing the word for at least 3 or 4 seconds, preferably longer, while maintaining eye contact with that one person. They may sing the word deep, or high, vibrato or steady; the note doesn't matter. What matters is that they let themselves and their feelings lead the sound of the word they are singing. Then, once they've sung that word, they move onto the next person in the line and sing the following word of the song, 'twinkle'. This may sound similar or entirely different from the previous word. The student must stay still with no arm movements while singing each word. Often tears are the first emotion released during this exercise; this is a very good reaction! Explain to the students beforehand that tears are a good sign, signalling that a block is being released. However, forced tears are not good; the emotion has to be real and well up from inside the actor authentically.

It's also important that the audience sitting in the line watching returns the eye contact when they are the one being looked at. They should also stay as still and as neutral as possible; even if the person doing the song exercise starts crying or laughing, they should do their best not to react.

Variation: If the person doing the song exercise seems particularly blocked, it can be good to do exactly the same as above but with the teacher calling out movements that the student does to accompany the sound. Movements can include marching, hopping, skipping, doing ballet or moving the torso side to side while standing still.

Tip: Make sure the group has been thoroughly warmed up vocally.

The aim: To vocally unblock students so that they have more freedom in the voice.

3 MOVEMENT

Introduction

The actor needs to learn how to move in an adaptable way. Freedom of movement is key to this, and related exercises for releasing tension can be found in Chapter 1, 'Relaxation and Focus'.

It's important that the actor feels comfortable in their own skin and confident to move freely and with ease so that they can add the movements of other characters onto their own. In this chapter, many of the exercises are playful in order to help students with the transition from relaxing the body to applying new ways of moving.

People consciously and unconsciously communicate feelings, statuses and attitudes through their body language and movement, and more will be covered on body language in Chapter 9, 'Physicalizing Characters'. The exercises in this chapter are designed to help students become more playful and uninhibited while practising new movements. Many of the exercises in this chapter are ideal for a group warm-up.

3.1 Lead with your …

A fun warm-up game that can inspire the creation of some interesting characters.

Age: 8 plus.
Skills: Creating a character, imagination, movement and mime.
Participants: This exercise can be done alone or in a group.
Time: 5–15 minutes (depending on the age group).
You'll need: A room big enough for students to walk around in.
How to: The students walk around the room. Ask them to become aware of their walk, to think about whether any part of their body is leading and, if it is, to adjust it so that the walk is neutral.

Now explain that you will call out a body part that students are to lead with. Let's start with the nose, for example. Now the students walk around the room leading with their nose. It's as if someone has a piece of string attached to their nose and this string is being pulled. Ask the students to think about what type of character might lead with their nose. A nosy neighbour perhaps who likes to gossip? Or a mean schoolteacher who doesn't like children? Let the students have fun creating characters who lead with their nose. They should do this silently and only use body language to communicate these characters.

Now change the body part to lead with – the hips perhaps. Have the students walk around leading with their hips for a few moments and now ask them to walk around as a character who might walk like that. A supermodel maybe? Or a rapper? Or an arrogant businessman or woman? Play like this for a while, leading with many different body parts – the chest, the chin, the forehead, the stomach, etc. Once this is finished, the teacher can ask the class to sit down and see if any volunteers would like to show some of the characters they have created.

Variation one: Asks students to choose one of the characters they just created and to walk around the room as that character. The room will fill with a variety of different characters, some leading with their hips, some with their foreheads and others with their stomachs. Ask students questions as they walk around as their character and encourage them to answer the questions in their head. Questions might include: 'What's your name?' 'Where do you live?' 'Do you have family and if so who's in it?' 'What makes you happy?' 'What makes you angry?' 'Where do you see yourself in 10 years' time?' 'Do you have any physical pain in your body from the way you hold yourself?' 'If you could change one thing about the world, what would it be?' Explain to students that now they know more about their characters; they can think about how this affects the character's movement. For example, if in reaction to the question 'What makes you angry?' the actor decided the answer for their character was strangers. The actor may now walk around with closed and defensive body language avoiding others as they pass them.

Variation two: Now the students have a character to play with; they can use these characters for a variety of scenes or improvisation exercises. Improvisation exercises which work well for this include: 'I'm sorry I ...' and 'I got you this present' (Chapter 4); 'Taxi driver with given circumstances' (Chapter 5); 'Broken-down lift' (Chapter 6); 'Hospital queue' and 'A job interview' (Chapter 7); and 'The letter', 'What are you doing?' and 'Park bench' (Chapter 8).

Tip: Start off with the easiest body parts first (the nose and chin) and then move onto the parts that may make students feel more self-conscious (the chests and hips).

The aim: For students to create characters through movement.

3.2 Elbow to elbow

A simple physical warm-up exercise.

Age: 8 plus.
Skills: Movement, energy, spatial awareness and group awareness.
Participants: Needs to be done in a group of five or more.
Time: 5–10 minutes.
You'll need: A room big enough for students to walk around in at a fast pace.
How to: The students walk around the room at a brisk speed, making sure they don't bump into anyone or anything. Encourage the students to use up all of the space in the room and to change direction frequently. The teacher will call out a body part. Let's say 'elbow' to start with, and the students run towards someone and touch their elbow to someone else's elbow. This doesn't have to be done in pairs; there can be groups of three or more touching elbows, although you will find the group will naturally gravitate into pairs. After everyone has found an elbow to touch their elbow with, the teacher calls 'go' and the students walk around the room again. After a few moments, the teacher calls out another body part – hand, for example – and the students race to touch their hand to someone else's hand. Good body parts to call include knee, hand, thumb, foot, shoulder, back, little finger, wrist and ankle. Be careful not to call out any inappropriate body parts.
Tip: Don't let anyone feel left out in this game. If someone is hovering around feeling like they can't join a pair who are already touching elbows, encourage them to go over and make a three. This game is about inclusion, not exclusion.
The aim: To warm students up physically.

3.3 Pass the shake

A simple physical warm-up exercise.

Age: 8 plus.
Skills: Movement, energy and group awareness.
Participants: Needs to be done in a group of five or more.
Time: 5–10 minutes.
You'll need: A room students can stand in a circle in.
How to: Students stand in a circle, and one person starts the game by shaking or wiggling one part of their body quite vigorously. This can be the hand, foot, elbow, head, stomach or any other suitable body part. The student shakes or wiggles this body part – let's say they choose the foot – and then they direct the shake at someone else in the circle. The person who the shake was aimed at starts shaking the same body part, the foot in this case. They shake it for a few

moments and then they start to shake another part of their body – let's say the eyelids, for example. This person will wiggle their eyelids for a few moments and then aim it at someone else in the circle and then that person will start shaking their eyelids for a few moments and then change the shake to another part of their body and so on. The game continues like this. Note that once the person has passed the shake onto someone else, they can stop shaking.

Tip: Before starting this game, instruct the whole group to shake one body part at a time all together to warm them up, including the leg, an arm, the head, a foot, a hand and so on.

The aim: To encourage students to loosen up physically.

3.4 Animal movement

A movement exercise where students take on some of the physicality of animals to inspire new ways of moving. Younger students particularly enjoy this exercise.

Age: 8 plus.
Skills: Imagination and movement.
Participants: This exercise can be done alone or in a group.
Time: 10–20 minutes.
You'll need: A room big enough for students to move around in.
How to: Many actors use animals to inspire themselves in their work in character building and movement. One classic direction in an audition is 'do your monologue again but this time with the movement of a lion'. (Or any other animal the audition panel feels is suited to the character.)

Ask the students to walk around the room and tell them that when you call out an animal, they need to respond by physically embodying that animal. They should go for it completely, becoming animal-like and unafraid of what others might think. There is no need to add any vocalization to the animal. The teacher can call out any animal – lion, puppy, fox, swan, mouse, gorilla, elephant, etc. If the teacher starts with a lion, ask the students to really think about how that particular animal moves. Is the animal slow or fast? Predatory or submissive? How do they move their spines? Their heads? Where does their centre of energy come from? Younger children tend to be particularly good at this exercise and can become any animal without much thought or any inhibitions. Teenagers might need a bit more encouraging and energy thrown at them by the teacher to participate fully.

Once the class has done this for about 5 minutes, explain that you would like them to walk around the room as humans but still displaying the traits of the animal called out. If, for example, the teacher calls out 'lion', the students will walk around on two legs, but they will adapt their movement to be more lion-like – perhaps slowing down, or becoming slightly aggressive, or flicking their hair every so often.

Tip: Encourage students to either go to the zoo or watch a wildlife programme and to really study the movement of the animal.

The aim: To encourage students to move their bodies in new and imaginative ways without any inhibitions.

3.5 Tableaux

A great exercise for breaking the ice and for a group to get to know each other while loosening up their bodies.

Age: 8 plus.
Skills: Teamwork, communicative skills, awareness and movement.
Participants: This exercise needs to be done in groups of four or five.
Time: 10–15 minutes.
You'll need: A space big enough for students to walk around in.
How to: Ask students to get into groups of four or five. Explain that when you call out something, as a team the group needs to create a frozen picture, and they have 10 seconds to do so. The teacher can call out anything – a setting, a scene, an emotion, an object – and then the teacher counts down from ten as the students arrange themselves into a tableau. Once they are in the tableau, the teacher can pick one and ask the rest of the class to come and have a look at it. Encourage students to use their bodies and faces to communicate their idea. Tableau ideas might include the jungle, the beach, an office, monster school, excitement, a fruit bowl, the colour red or the bathroom.
Variation: Have a pile of props in the centre of the room, and these can be used for inspiration for the tableaux. When the teacher says 'go', the group can take one prop and create a tableau to go with it.
Tip: Encourage students to use different levels with some perhaps lying down, others sitting and others standing.
The aim: For students to work as a team, to become less self-conscious and to be creative with movement.

3.6 Guess the leader

A fun warm-up game where one student leads the movement and the rest of the group follow, while another student has to guess which person is the leader.

Age: 8 plus.
Skills: Confidence, group awareness and trust.
Participants: A group of five or more.
Time: 10–15 minutes.
You'll need: A group of students to stand in a circle.

How to: Students stand in a circle, and one volunteer leaves the room (or turns their back and closes their eyes). Let's call this volunteer Yulia. Once Yulia cannot see or hear what the group is doing, another volunteer is chosen; let's call him Brad. Brad will stay where he is in the circle. The whole class must know that Brad is now the leader and they will have to follow his movements but in a way that means Yulia cannot detect who the leader is.

Once Yulia returns, she stands in the centre of the circle. Brad will very slowly and carefully start moving, perhaps bringing one arm up or tilting his head. The whole group will copy his movement, and the whole circle will hopefully appear as if it is moving as one. Yulia has to try and guess who the leader is; she only gets three guesses. Brad can move as he likes, but he will find that the slower the movements, the less likely he is to get found out by Yulia.

Tip: Encourage students not to stare at the leader so that it isn't too obvious.

The aim: For students to become very aware of their own movements and the movements of the group.

3.7 Exploring the centre of energy

A subtle movement exercise to help students become more mindful of their movements.

Age: 8 plus.
Skills: Creating a character, imagination, movement and mindfulness.
Participants: This exercise can be done alone or in a group.
Time: 5–15 minutes.
You'll need: A room big enough for students to walk around in.
How to: As students walk around the room, ask them to become aware of any parts of their bodies they think they hold energy in; often this can be the part of the body people like about themselves. Perhaps it's the eyes, lips, or stomach, or somewhere else. Now explain that different people tend to hold their centre of energy in a particular place in their body. Students are now going to walk around the room imagining that their centre of energy is in different places in their body. Let's start with the eyes: imagine the eyes are the centre of energy in the body and see how that might change how the student moves. They may open them wider, move the eyes around the room more, flutter their eyelids and express their wants and feelings through their eyes. But if the centre of the energy were in the hands, for example, the actor may gesture a lot with their hands and use their hands frequently and elaborately during speech. Changing the centre of energy can completely change the way someone holds themselves. For someone who holds their centre of energy in their lips, for example, they may pout, smile a lot and use them as their primary source of communication.

Call out different centres of energy every few minutes – the hips, stomach, chest, hands, shoulders, face, eyes, lips and tongue – and students walk around exploring what it would be like to hold energy in those parts of the body. Ask students to do a quick greeting with one another as they pass each other so that they can explore how where the centre of energy is held affects their interactions with others.

Variation one: Ask students to choose one of the characters they just created and to walk around the room as that character. The room will fill with a variety of different characters, some with the centre of energy in their lips, some with it in their eyebrows and others in their stomachs. Ask students questions as they walk around as their character and encourage them to answer the questions in their head. Questions might include: 'What's your name?' 'Where do you live?' 'Do you have family and if so who's in it?' 'What makes you happy?' 'What makes you angry?' 'Where do you see yourself in 10 years time?' 'What's your favourite feature?'

Variation two: Now the students have a character to play with; they can use these characters for a variety of scenes or improvisation exercises. Improvisation exercises which work well for this include: 'I'm sorry I ...' and 'I got you this present' (Chapter 4); 'Taxi driver with given circumstances' (Chapter 5); 'Broken-down lift' (Chapter 6); 'Hospital queue' and 'A job interview' (Chapter 7); and 'The letter', 'What are you doing?' and 'Park bench' (Chapter 8).

Tip: The centre of energy is very different to tension. When talking about energy, it is meant in a very positive way, for example, how a wizard might hold his energy in his finger tips as he rubs them together just before using his magic wand.

The aim: For students to think about movement in an internal way and to communicate characters subtly with the body.

3.8 Animal dinner party

A fun game where students take on the characteristics of an animal and then have to find their mate.

Age: 8 plus.
Skills: Group awareness, social skills, communicative skills, imagination and creativity.
Participants: This exercise needs to be done in a group of ten or more.
Time: 10–15 minutes.
You'll need: A room to host an imaginary party. It's good to lay out an imaginary food table for this exercise, as well as some chairs, and maybe even play some party music in the background. You'll also need pens and paper. If you want to go all out and make yourself very popular, for a special treat, you could put some real food on the table!
How to: The teacher gives each student a piece of paper with the name of an animal on it, which the student keeps a secret. You should end up with two of

each animal in the group, so if there are thirty in the class, there will be fifteen different animals. If there is an odd number of students in the class, one student can be the host of the party and they are not given an animal.

Once the students know their animal, they can throw away their piece of paper. They will go to the party as a human but with the characteristics of the animal they've been given. They must not tell anyone their animal. They then talk to people at the party, asking questions to try to find their mate. So if you were given a piece of paper with 'swan' on, for example, you might be very graceful, a ballerina perhaps or a fashion designer, or you may even be related to royalty. Or, if you were a tiger, you might be drawn to the meat section of the buffet table and be very confident, perhaps a manager at a big business or a terrifying head teacher.

Encourage students to physically take on the characteristics of their animal and get them to stagger their entrance to the party. If the group is an even number, the teacher can be the host or can see if a student who is also an animal is happy to be the host. To liven things up, have students imagine a buffet table of food and play some music. Now students can socialize at the party as they try and find their mate. Once it looks like everyone has found their mate, stop the game and ask the students to tell each other which animal they are.

Tip: Explain to students that they don't have to take on all the traits of the animal, and it can be easier to focus on just one. For example, if they are assigned a lion, they may choose just to do the swishing of the mane.

The aim: To improve students' social skills and to encourage them to embody a new way of moving in an improvisation setting.

3.9 Favourite feature

An acting exercise to encourage the actor to move in new ways.

Age: 8 plus.
Skills: Creating a character, movement and mime.
Participants: This exercise can be done alone or in a group.
Time: 10–15 minutes.
You'll need: A room students can move around in.
How to: Start by asking students to walk around the room. Explain that when you call out a body part, the student is to imagine this is their favourite feature about themselves. Let's say the teacher calls out 'eyes'; the students will then walk around imagining that their eyes are their favourite feature. Now ask the students to all shake hands with another student and introduce themselves, still with their eyes as their favourite feature. People's movements are often influenced by what they like and dislike about themselves. If your favourite feature about yourself is your eyes, you may open them wide, make them expressive while you talk and be keen to make eye contact. Ask the students

to move around the room introducing themselves to as many different people as possible with their eyes as their favourite feature. Then after a few minutes, change the body part so that now the hands are their favourite feature. Carry on like this, changing the favourite feature every so often. Other body parts may include the feet, waist, collarbone, lips and hair. When working with under-18s, it is important to avoid the more sexual areas of the body in this exercise.

Variation one: What you don't like about yourself can also influence movement. A fun variation of the above exercise is to call out a body part that the student can imagine they don't like about themselves. So if you called 'lips', for example, the actor would imagine they don't like their lips; they might keep touching and covering their lips when introducing themselves, or they might bite their lips or turn their head down slightly to draw attention away from their lips.

Variation two: Another variation is to do one favourite feature and one feature you don't like about yourself at the same time. For example, 'you like your hair, but you dislike your nose'.

Tip: Ask students to think about their own movement in everyday life and how their favourite and least favourite features about themselves affect their movement. However, don't ask them to share this information with the class as it's private.

Aim: For students to explore how the way a character thinks about themselves affects their movements.

3.10 Entering an audition

A game to help students gain confidence in an audition.

Age: 8 plus.
Skills: Movement, professionalism, audition skills and social skills.
Participants: This exercise needs to be done in a group of ten or more.
Time: 10–15 minutes.
You'll need: A room with a table and four chairs behind it and one chair placed centre stage in front of the table.
How to: Explain to the students that how they hold themselves when they walk into an audition is very important. If they walk into the audition in an apologetic or defensive way, audition panels will instantly be put off. Part of the audition is how the actor walks into the audition room before they've even started their reading, scene or monologue.

Set out a room as if it is an audition. Lay a table out at one end of the room with four people sitting behind it, and opposite this set up an empty chair. Sit the class near the audition panel. Ask one student (the auditionee) to leave the room and then re-enter the room as if this were at an audition. They have to walk from the door to sitting down on the chair opposite the audition panel.

Explain that the auditionee needs to enter the room with neutral but confident body language. Also encourage the practising auditionee to acknowledge the audition panel as they enter with a graceful nod and hello. Explain to students that they must never apologize to an audition panel or make excuses about having a cold or not having time to learn lines. The auditionee must always enter in a calm, professional, confident and present way.

Once you start practising this, it will become clear that many students, without even realizing it, walk over to the chair tugging at their clothes, twiddling their fingers, biting their bottom lip and so on. Each time a student does something that does not constitute neutral/confident body language, ask them to re-enter the room. You may ask some students to re-enter eight, nine or ten times. That's okay unless they start looking distressed; if that happens, ask them if they'd like to stop the exercise and respect their decision. Some students will find this practice very difficult and may start messing around and making jokes. Keep going with these students until they can enter the room naturally and with confidence. Never force someone to practise this exercise.

Tip: It's fun if the teacher can practise *teacher in role* here and become the person on the audition panel. If the teacher creates an interesting character for the person sat on the audition panel, this exercise will become more fun and entertaining.

The aim: For students to learn how to enter an audition room without any inhibitions or tensions in the body.

4 UNBLOCKING PERFORMERS

Introduction

Part of the actor's training is to learn how to respond to creative intuition without being afraid of what others think. While teaching children and young people, one of the biggest obstacles to creativity is that too many youngsters are afraid to shine in front of their classmates. This can be for a number of reasons, but it's the drama teacher's job to create a safe space where students have the confidence to shine and be their true selves. There's some advice in the introduction on how to create a safe space.

In this chapter I provide exercises that are fun, simple and good for building improvisation skills and confidence. In order to unblock students, it's important that neither the teacher nor anyone else in the group is negative about any idea or improvisation. All ideas should be praised (unless the idea causes another student harm). The drama group should be trained by the teacher to praise each other, to accept all ideas and to fully go with any suggestion.

The unblocked actor can perform from the subconscious and listen to their intuition; this is what all actors should be aiming for. Improvisation is one of the best practices for obtaining this state; therefore, this chapter is made up of 100 per cent improvisation exercises.

4.1 Pass the face

A simple warm-up game where students look at one another as they pass a facial expression around the circle.

Age: 8 plus.
Skills: Communicative skills, imagination, confidence and improvisation.
Participants: A group of five or more.

Time: 5–10 minutes.

You'll need: A group of students to sit in a circle.

How to: Ask students to sit in a circle and explain that a facial expression is going to be passed around the circle. This can be any expression: sad, happy, worried, afraid, excited or any other feeling that the teacher or group can think of. Let's start with excited. One student will start: they give an excited look to the person sitting next to them. The person they are sitting next to will then fill with excitement and pass the excited look to the next person in the circle. The excited look gets passed around the circle until everyone has received and passed on the excited look.

Tip: Ask students to make eye contact with the person they are passing the face to.

The aim: For students to become comfortable with expressing an emotion and then showing this.

4.2 Honey, I love you

A fun warm-up game where students are not allowed to smile when someone approaches them and says in a humorous way, 'Honey, I love you.'

Age: 8 plus.

Skills: Communicative skills, imagination, confidence, self-control, group awareness and improvisation.

Participants: A group of five or more.

Time: 10–15 minutes.

You'll need: A group of students to stand in a circle.

How to: Students stand in a circle, and one student volunteers and stands in the centre; let's call her Carolina. Carolina approaches one person in the circle and says, 'Honey, I love you!' It's Carolina's aim to make this person laugh, so she may say this in a funny way, perhaps by getting down on one knee and saying it in a silly voice or she may do a funny little dance. The person she says 'Honey, I love you!' to – let's call her Eden – is not allowed to smile and, with a completely straight face, she has to reply with 'Honey, I love you too, but I just can't smile.' If Eden smiles, she needs to go into the centre of the circle and take Carolina's place and Carolina stands in the circle, while Eden chooses a new person to say 'Honey, I love you!'. However, if Eden manages to keep a straight face, Carolina stays where she is in the circle and has to find someone else to say 'Honey, I love you!'.

Tip: Ask students not to make physical contact in this exercise as it has the potential to go too far in this exercise.

The aim: To loosen students up and encourage them to have fun, while learning how to control the face by not smiling.

4.3 Sausages

A fun game where students have to practise not smiling – perfect for a warm-up or cool-down.

Age: 8 plus.
Skills: Listening, communicative skills, self-control and focus.
Participants: This exercise can be practised with two participants, but five or more are preferable.
Time: 5–15 minutes.
You'll need: A chair centre stage and for the students to sit in front of this like an audience.
How to: The teacher asks everybody to sit as an audience facing one chair that is set centre stage. A volunteer will sit on that chair. When sitting on the chair, you are not allowed to smile or cover your face. The aim is to keep a neutral expression while sitting on the chair. Members of the audience put up their hands to ask a question, and the student on the chair will point to the person who is to ask the question. The questions can be anything: 'What's your favourite food?', 'What is your favourite book?' or 'What do you brush your teeth with?' The only answer the person on the chair is allowed to give is 'sausages'. And they must keep a straight face. If the person on the chair smiles or laughs, then they come off the chair and the person who asked the question that made them break sits on the chair and becomes the questioner with the straight face.
Variation: This game can be played with another word that isn't 'sausages'. 'Monkeys', 'cheese' and 'slime' all work too. If choosing another word, don't use the name of someone in the class.
Tip: The person who is sat on the chair should not cover their face or tense their lips to try and hide a smile. They should maintain a relaxed, blank and tension-free expression.
The aim: For students to learn how to control their facial expressions and reactions in times of difficulty.

4.4 Yes, let's!

A fast-paced group improvisation exercise.

Age: 8 plus.
Skills: Listening, spontaneity, imagination and improvisation.
Participants: This exercise needs to be practised in a group of five or more.
Time: 5–10 minutes.
You'll need: A space big enough for students to walk around in.

How to: Ask the students to stand in a space in the room and then initiate an action by saying something like 'Let's bake a cake.' Ask the class to reply with 'Yes, let's!' and then they will all pretend to bake a cake. The students can shout out any idea they like; nothing is too crazy. Perhaps someone might call out:

'Let's wash a lion!'

'Yes, let's!' the class will call out.

And everyone will wash a lion.

Then someone might call, 'Let's all be aeroplanes.'

'Yes, let's!' the class will call out.

And everyone will pretend to be aeroplanes. The game continues like this.

Theming: This game can be themed. Let's imagine that you are leading a fairy-tale workshop. In this case, the game could be played as above, but instead of the suggestions being random, they are suggestions which meet the theme fairy tales. For example, someone might say, 'Let's all climb a beanstalk.' The class is to reply with 'Yes, let's!' and then they will all pretend to climb a beanstalk. The students can shout out any idea they like; nothing is too crazy, but ask them to keep to the fairy-tale theme. Perhaps someone else might call out:

'Let's blow down the little pig's house.'

'Yes, let's!' the class will call out.

And everyone will blow down the little pig's house.

Then someone might call, 'Let's clean the fireplace.'

'Yes, let's!' the class will call out.

And everyone will pretend to clean the fireplace. The game continues like this.

Tip: For younger students or/and groups that are lively, it's a good idea for the teacher to stop the class with a signal for silence and then ask students to put their hands up if they have a suggestion for the next 'Yes, let's!' idea. This way the student calling the idea will be heard and a mixture of students will get to make suggestions. Encourage the quieter members of the group to contribute ideas too.

The aim: For all improvisation ideas to be accepted and acted on with the aim of loosening up students and creating a space where they feel safe to improvise in.

4.5 Acting to music

An exercise where students allow music to affect their performance.

Age: 8 plus.

Skills: Listening, spontaneity, imagination and intuition.

Participants: This exercise can be done alone or in a group.

Time: 10–15 minutes.

You'll need: A device to play music on; a good-quality speake~~r~~
Five to ten pieces of emotive music with no vocals; classical
soundtracks work best. A space for students to walk around
to the music.

How to: Ask the students to lie down on the floor, and if there~~ ~~
relaxation exercise from Chapter 1. Once the students are lying down, exp~~ ~~
to them that you are going to play a piece of music and that it's okay to let the
music affect them. Once the music begins to play, students can listen to it lying
down for about 30 seconds or more, and when they are ready, they can stand
up and move around the room in response to how the music is making them
feel. Explain that there is no right or wrong with this exercise and that music
can trigger all kinds of different feelings. The student is to move and react to the
feelings it triggers in any way they feel is right. The music may inspire them to
be a wizard skipping to wizard school, to walk through a cave terrified or to sit
quietly reflecting on happier times. Whatever the music inspires, the students
must follow their intuition and go with that, not paying attention to anyone else
in the group. It is during this exercise that I have seen many of my students give
their best ever acting performances!

Once all the tracks have been played, ask if any students would like to
show some of the work they have just created, and play the music again for
their performance. They may or may not want to tell the group what their
performance was about; the teacher can leave that up to the student.

When the exercise is over, explain that many professional actors use music
to get them into character, and actors can often be found listening to music
just before they go on set or on stage. When students have a character they are
working on, encourage them to come up with a playlist for that character.

Variation: Spilt the group into teams of four or five and play a short piece of music.
Now give the students 10 to 15 minutes to create a short scene inspired by this
piece of music.

Tip: The teacher should pick a good variety of emotive music for this exercise; film
soundtracks are my favourite. Film soundtracks have a magical way of fully
transporting the actor to an imaginative place. Some of my favourite composers
for this exercise include John Williams, Hans Zimmer, James Newton Howard,
Pyotr Ilyich Tchaikovsky and Danny Elfman. Avoid music with lyrics as they
can be too leading.

The aim: To use music to encourage students to act from a place of feeling.

4.6 I'm sorry I …

A fast-paced improvisation exercise perfect for a group warm-up.

Age: 8 plus.
Skills: Listening, spontaneity, imagination and improvisation.

Participants: This needs to be done in a group of five or more.

Time: 10–15 minutes.

You'll need: A room big enough to sit in a circle.

How to: The group sits in a circle, and one person – let's call her Rania – starts by standing up. Rania approaches a person sitting in the circle, and she apologizes for something. Let's say she approaches Maya. Rania might be very sorry because she has lost Maya's pet dog, she's smashed Maya's phone or she's cast an irreversible spell on Maya's brother. Maya can react in any way she likes. She could be sad, cross or maybe even pleased about the accident. What's vital here is that whatever Rania is apologizing for, Maya goes along with it. Once the short improvisation comes to an end, Maya will then pick someone else in the circle and approach them to apologize for something. Maya might go over to Vadim, for example, and apologize for getting mud on his coat. But if Vadim asks to pass, that's okay; Maya can pick someone else. Improvisation must never be forced onto anyone as that could put them off for life. Chances are if Vadim is given a few weeks in class just to watch, in a few weeks' time, he will join in with an improvisation exercise of his own accord once he's ready.

Tip: It can be fun when students play this game in character. Explain to students that they can be any character they like – a school teacher, princess or astronaut. Once they think of a character, it is likely to give them inspiration for something to be sorry for.

The aim: To encourage students to improvise with spontaneity and to not block one another.

4.7 I got you this present!

A fast-paced improvisation exercise perfect for a group warm-up.

Age: 8 plus.

Skills: Listening, spontaneity, imagination and improvisation.

Participants: This needs to be done in a group of five or more.

Time: 10–15 minutes.

You'll need: A room big enough to sit in a circle.

How to: The group sits in a circle, and one person – let's say Jay – starts by standing up and approaching someone else in the circle – let's call them Youssef. Jay gives Youssef a present. The gift can be anything, maybe some smelly used socks, a dragon's egg or a motorbike. Youssef, who is receiving the gift, can react in any way he likes. He may love the gift, hate it or be astounded. What's vital here is that whatever the giver gives, the other person goes along with it. Once the short improvisation comes to an end, Youssef will pick someone else in the circle and approach them with a different gift. If Youssef picks someone and they ask to pass, that's okay. Ask Youssef to pick someone else.

Variation: For advanced students, they can play the game as above, but instead of the giver giving a physical object, they can give something that isn't in a gift. For example, a parking ticket, exam results, a compliment or a telling off.

Tip: Explain to students that they really need to imagine the physical object in their hands and physically hand it over to the receiver. The receiver needs to physically take it, and it should always be clear who is holding the object through the actor's use of mime. Props shouldn't be used for this exercise.

The aim: To encourage students to improvise with spontaneity and to not block one another.

4.8 Freeze!

A popular improvisation game where anything can happen!

Age: 8 plus.

Skills: Listening, spontaneity, imagination, storytelling, teamwork and improvisation.

Participants: This needs to be done in a group of five or more.

Time: 10–15 minutes.

You'll need: A room big enough to sit in a circle.

How to: Sit the class down as an audience and set up a space to be used as the 'stage'. Ask two volunteers to step onto the stage. They may improvise any scene they like. Explain that it's a good idea to know the location and what type of character you are and then to fully commit to this and improvise. For example, one might turn to the other and say, 'I'm fed up with this bus always being late.' This way the other person in the improvisation knows they are at a bus stop and can go along with that idea. The pair on stage may improvise for 30 seconds or a few minutes.

The two improvisers will freeze when someone in the audience claps their hands and shouts, 'Freeze'. The person who called out will now walk onto the stage and tap the person they want to leave on the shoulder. The person who is tapped will leave and the new improviser will take the position they were frozen in. This new person joining the improvisation will start a new idea. Say, for example, in the freeze they were looking at their watches, they may start the new improvisation by looking at their watch and saying, 'What time do you call this young lady? It's a school night!'

The exercise continues like this with audience members calling out freeze when they would like to have a turn on stage. Explain to the students that if the two improvisers look like they are struggling, someone should call 'freeze' to help them out/put them out of their misery! Also explain that if the improvisation is going very well, they shouldn't call out 'freeze'; instead, they should let everyone enjoy the magic that's being created on stage. It's also important to make it clear that no idea is too 'silly'; all ideas are welcome.

Whether it be an improvisation of the first astronauts walking on Mars or a snail trying to cross a busy road, all ideas are welcome. A nice touch to help students with confidence is to encourage the audience to applaud each time a performer leaves the stage.

Variation: The teacher can lay props out, the students can use these for the improvisation and/or the audience can call out the location of the improvisation just before each improvisation begins. Once the two actors are in their frozen positions ready to start, the teacher can ask one member of the audience to provide a location for the improvisation, again stating that no idea is too silly. Ideas may include the beach, the zoo, the head teacher's office, a space ship, superhero school or the set of *Doctor Who*.

Tip: For a younger or more excitable class, it's best the teacher calls out 'freeze' rather than the students.

The aim: For students to learn how to accept all ideas in improvisation and to fully commit to their intuition and imagination.

4.9 Lie about how you got here

A fun storytelling warm-up game.

Age: 8 plus.
Skills: Listening, storytelling, creativity and communicative skills.
Participants: This exercise can be practised with two participants, but five or more are preferable.
Time: 5–15 minutes.
You'll need: A space big enough for students to sit in a circle.
How to: The students sit in a circle, and the teacher makes up a story about how they got to class. Perhaps the teacher put the car keys into the ignition, the car made some strange jolting noises, then there was a very weird sulphur smell and all of a sudden purple smoke started pouring out of the exhaust pipe. Then there was a loud bang; some huge green wings sprouted out of the car and the teacher flew to class waving at all the passers-by! After telling a short story, explain that students are to tell a lie about how they got to class today. No idea is too wacky. Encourage every student to have a turn, although don't force them. Explain that even a very short story is fine. Perhaps they got to class on roller skates. Longer stories are fine too. Anything goes in this exercise. Explain to the students that good eye contact is key to telling a good story, and while telling the story, they should try and make eye contact with the people in the circle.

Variation: Split the group up into groups of three or four and give them 10 to 15 minutes to practise a short scene. Get one person to tell the story of how they got to class today and the other two or three people to act it out.

Tip: Encourage students not to rush their stories while telling them and ask them to use pauses while they are telling a story as it is often a dramatic pause which can really draw an audience in.

The aim: To encourage students to trust their imaginations and to improve their storytelling techniques.

4.10 Status

A fun acting exercise where students play at being people with different statuses.

Age: 8 plus.
Skills: Listening, spontaneity, imagination, social skills and improvisation.
Participants: This needs to be practised in pairs.
Time: 10–20 minutes.
You'll need: A space where students can stand in a room in pairs and improvise.
How to: Ask the students to get into pairs. Name one in the pair A and the other B. A will start by being a person with high status and B will be someone with low status. For example, A might be a queen and B a servant. Or A could be someone interviewing people for a job and B an interviewee. It is important to note that a job title doesn't necessarily give someone higher status. For example, A could play the higher status as a student and B the lower status as a teacher, perhaps because it's the teacher's first day at school and B is a student testing the teacher's boundaries. Ask the students to come up with a 1- or 2-minute improvisation where A has higher status than B.

Now ask the partners to swap over so that B has a turn being the person with higher status and A the lower status. Examples include: B could be the head cheerleader and A is trying out for the squad. Or B is a cleaner who has just spotted her boss, person A, stealing money from the safe.

Once the actors in the pair have both had a turn at playing with both statuses, ask them to choose the improvisation they thought worked best, then ask them to practise once more and then show these to the rest of the class.

Variation: Ask the students to walk around the room and explain that when you call out the number 1, they will walk around the room as someone with a very low status and when you call out number 10, they will walk around the room as someone with a very high status. Number 3 will be someone with medium/low status, number 7 someone with medium/high status and so on. Ask the students to think about what situation they are in for them to have that particular status and how that may change how they move and behave. If the students are walking around as number 10, the highest status, perhaps they are a celebrity waving to their fans, a head teacher about to take an assembly or the president about to sign an important document. Or if students are walking around as number 1, perhaps they are a slave being forced onto a ship, a child at school being picked on by older kids or a student being told off for not doing their homework.

Tip: Explain to students that they should be careful not to stereotype people with certain jobs into a low or high status. It should be the situation that determines the statuses at play. For example, an office worker could have a higher status over her boss if she wants to leave her job but he really wants her to stay.

The aim: For students to think about how their gestures and behaviours change depending on the status of their character in a certain situation.

4.11 Meisner acting technique – the repetition exercise

A well-known exercise in which two students observe each other; this is taught in many drama schools and acting classes.

Age: 11 plus.

Skills: Acceptance, concentration, communicative skills, confidence, intuition, listening and spontaneity.

Participants: Students will need to work in pairs.

Time: 10–15 minutes.

You'll need: A room where students can stand together in pairs and talk to one another.

Background: The Meisner acting technique is a technique developed by Sanford Meisner. The technique teaches the actor to think less, react to stimuli and get in touch with their instinct. If you're teaching this technique, you should first create a safe space for your students to work in. The facilitator should explain that mistakes are okay and polished and well thought-out performances are discouraged. The technique should be liberating, encouraging the performer not to think but instead to just do. Improvisation plays an important role in Meisner training as it allows the student to bring spontaneity into the scene.

Meisner believes that the actor must do what the character does: if the character is listening, the actor must really listen. The actor doesn't pretend to listen; they really listen and they really react. Meisner's most famous exercise is the repetition exercise, which trains actors to respond 'truthfully' and encourages them not to think but instead to respond to circumstance.

How to: For this repetition exercise, two actors sit or stand facing each other. One person – let's say her name is Hannah – says a phrase about how the other person looks or behaves; for example, 'You're wearing a black top.' The other person – let's call him Tyron – responds by repeating the phrase, but he would replace the word 'you', with 'I'; so Tyron would say, 'I'm wearing a black top.' The conversation carries on like this with one person making observations and the other repeating the observations back to them. Here's an example:

Hannah   You're wearing bandana.

Tyron   I am wearing a bandana.

Hannah   You scratched your eyebrow.

Tyron   I scratched my eyebrow.

Hannah   You smiled.

Tyron   I smiled.

Before starting, make it clear to students that the comments should be appropriate and never unkind; for example, 'You have a big nose' would be unacceptable. Also there shouldn't be any judgement in the observational phrase; for example, 'You look tired' would be a judgement and not a fact.

Let the students have a conversation in the vein of the example above for about 5 minutes, and then ask the pairs to swap over. So Tyron would observe and Hannah would repeat. For example:

Tyron   You have curly hair.

Hannah   I have curly hair.

Tyron   You're standing up.

Hannah   I'm standing up.

Tyron   You sniffed.

Hannah   I sniffed.

Variation: The above can also be practised with imagined given circumstances. For example, maybe Hannah's given circumstance could be that she is very cold and Tyron's could be that he is in a hurry as he has a dentist appointment. The same as above would be played out, but the two actors would now also be acting out given circumstances.

Tip: Explain to students that their focus should be entirely on themselves and the person they are working with. They should not bring their attention out of the scene by looking around the room or at something else.

The aim: To teach the students to be in the now and to follow their intuition. Meisner's principles of listening, responding and being in the moment are key to this exercise. By doing this exercise, the aim is for the actor to stop thinking about what to say and do and to respond to the other actor more freely and spontaneously.

5 GIVEN CIRCUMSTANCES

Introduction

The term 'given circumstances' was coined by Konstantin Stanislavsky in the first half of the twentieth century when he was at the Moscow Art Theatre. 'Given circumstances' refers to the environmental, historical and situational conditions a character finds themselves in. All actors should research their character's given circumstances, and even when the actor is not consciously thinking about them, the hope is that this learning will show up subconsciously in their performance.

For Stanislavsky, six questions make up a character's given circumstances:

- Who?
- When?
- Where?
- Why?
- For what reason?
- How?

The given circumstances are drawn from everything that can be found in the script, the physical conditions of the actual production, plus the circumstances created by the actors' and directors' imaginations. The answers to the first three of the six questions – who, when and where – are normally provided by the writer of the play or script and the surrounding research. The last three questions – why, for what reason and how – tend to be answered by the actors and directors.

Stanislavski describes the given circumstances as

- the story of the play;
- facts, events, epoch, time and place of action;

- the conditions of life for the character;
- the actors' and directors' interpretations;
- the arrangement of the set and props (*mise-en-scène*);
- the details of production: sets, costumes, lighting and sound.

The given circumstances are what springboard the imagination to Stanislavsky's 'magic if'.

Whenever an actor is given a character to play, they should spend some time getting to know their character's given circumstances. If the actor knows these details, they are much more likely to perform a three-dimensional and authentic character. To know the given circumstances, the actor must first read the whole play, and if the play is an adaptation of a book, they should also read the book. However, students shouldn't develop the given circumstances from films or productions that already exist as these secondary sources of material have already been interpreted. It is important that given circumstances come from the writer of the script and/or book, research, the actor and the director, if applicable.

The renowned theatre practitioner Uta Hagen has a slightly different set of questions to assist the actor with given circumstances, which she lays out in her book, *Respect for Acting*. These include:

1 Who am I? Character.

2 What time is it? Century, year, season, day and minute.

3 Where am I? Country, city, neighbourhood, house, room, area of room.

4 What surrounds me? Animate and inanimate objects.

5 What are the given circumstances? Past, present, future and the events.

6 What are my relationships? Relation to total events, other characters and things.

7 What do I want? Character, main and immediate objectives.

8 What is in my way? Obstacles.

9 What do I do to get what I want? The action: physical and verbal.

It's a good idea for the actor to answer both Stanislavsky's and Hagen's questions as part of their character research.

In this chapter, I've included some fun acting exercises that allow students to play with the idea of given circumstances, plus I've included exercises from Uta Hagen's *Respect for Acting* and exercises that are often used in professional training.

5.1 Hot-seating with given circumstances

An exploratory exercise to help students create characters.

Age: 8 plus.
Skills: Communicative skills, intuition, listening, spontaneity, creating a character, imagination and character building.
Participants: Minimum of two students, but can be practised as a group.
Time: 10–20 minutes.
You'll need: A chair for one student to sit on and space for the rest of the class to sit in front of this chair.
How to: Place a chair (the hot seat) on a stage, or in an area similar to a stage, and sit the rest of the class down so that they are facing this chair.

Ask for a volunteer to sit on the hot seat. If you are working on a play or scripts in the class, these characters can be used in this exercise. If you're not working on anything in class, students can choose any character they want. This could be a character from a book, a film or even a made-up character.

Ask the student in the hot seat to think about their character and all of their given circumstances, including their age, name, job (if they have one), place that they live, their friends, family, likes, dislikes, fears and wants. Explain that the actor can make up all of this information and that there is no right or wrong in this exercise. The volunteer in the hot seat then answers questions from the audience in character. Explain that they are not to come out of character and that if they don't know the answer to a question, they can either make an answer up or say, in character, that they don't know.

The audience can ask any questions they like to try and get to know the character. Standard questions are great, such as 'Do you have any brothers or sisters?' 'What's your favourite food?' and 'Where do you live?', but also encourage students to ask a wider set of questions. Stanislavsky's and Hagen's lists of questions can be a good springboard for this exercise. For example, they could ask, 'Where did you grow up?' 'How would you describe yourself in three words?' and 'What are your weaknesses?'

Variation: It's also possible to play this game in pairs instead of putting students on a hot seat in front of the whole class. Pair work is more suited to a timid class.
Tip: Ask students to avoid saying 'I don't know', and instead encourage them to quickly make up an answer.
The aim: To encourage students to think about the many different sides to the character they are playing and to build up a background, backstory and deeper understanding of who their character is.

5.2 Creating given circumstances for fairy-tale characters

An academic and imaginative exercise to encourage students to create backstories for characters.

Age: 8 plus.
Skills: Spontaneity, creating a character, imagination and character building.
Participants: This exercise can be done alone or in a group.
Time: 10–20 minutes.
You'll need: A pen and paper for each student.
How to: Ask the students to think of one character from a fairy tale and a scene from the fairy tale featuring this character – for example, when Jack sells his cow Daisy, or when Snow White takes an apple from the disguised queen, or when the wolf talks to Little Red Riding Hood in the woods. Now ask the students to take that character and scene and to answer the questions below:

- What's the character's name?
- What are their hobbies?
- What don't they like?
- What are their favourite things?
- Do they have any enemies?
- How old are they?
- Where do they live?
- Who make up their family?
- Do they have any friends?
- How have they found themselves in the situation they are in?
- What are their surroundings like at the moment?
- Are they cold, hot, hungry, in a rush or in any pain?

Explain, or encourage in fact, before you begin that it's okay to make up the answers and that there is no right or wrong answer. Any interpretation is acceptable.

Variation one: After students have gathered all of this information on their character, they can put it into practice. Ask them to create short 5-minute improvisations in groups of three to four using their characters. It can be fun to have a group of characters from different fairy tales all together, and this provides a good base for a new and unique improvisation.

Variation two: This exercise can be practised with a different set of characters that are not fairy-tale characters. For an older, more advanced group, the same

exercise as above could be done with Shakespearean charac
from novels or characters from musicals.

Tip: Discourage students from overthinking or writing things do
them to approach given circumstances in a practical and in'

The aim: To give students basic knowledge of how to apply giv.
to characters.

5.3 Taxi driver with given circumstances

A fun improvisation game where students play out a scene in a taxi.

Age: 8 plus.

Skills: Communicative skills, intuition, listening, spontaneity, creating a character and imagination.

Participants: Minimum of two students; it can be practised as a group too.

Time: 10–20 minutes.

You'll need: Five chairs set out in the shape of a car.

How to: Set up five chairs, two as the front seats of a car and three as the back seats. Ask the class to sit down in front of the imaginary car as an audience. Ask two students who are happy to improvise to volunteer. One student will be the taxi driver and the other will hail the taxi and get into the car.

Ask the students to create a character by developing a set of given circumstances. For example, the taxi driver's given circumstances might be that they are at the end of a long shift, they have taken on extra hours to fund their son's university tuition and they are exhausted. The given circumstances of the person who is getting into the taxi might be that they have an audition at the other end of town, they are really hoping to get the part as it's for their favourite musical of all time and they need to warm up their voice. Students can choose any given circumstances they like; three is a pretty good number to start off with. Once they have their given circumstances, let them improvise the scene. When the improvisation looks as if it's drawing to a close, initiate an applause, praise the good points of the improvisation and ask two more students to come up on stage and have a go.

Variation one: Instead of students getting up on a stage and doing the improvisation straight away in front of the class, the teacher can give everyone 10 minutes to go away in pairs and practise a scene in private. Then each pair can show the polished improvisation to the class.

Variation two: This exercise can be practised in many different ways. It can be played without any given circumstances where students are given the freedom to improvise in any way they wish within the structure of the taxi driver exercise. Or it can be played with the two actors both playing an objective each (see the chapter on objectives) or with the two actors both playing an action each (see the chapter on actions). For advanced students, they can play the characters with given circumstances, an objective and an action.

: Explain/demonstrate that it's important to really imagine the car. If you're the person getting into the taxi, imagine opening the car door and putting on a seatbelt; if you're playing the taxi driver, steer, use a gear stick and hand break, and keep your eyes on the road.

The aim: To improve improvisation skills and show students how given circumstances can provide stimuli for an improvisation.

5.4 Packing a bag with given circumstances

An acting exercise where students do a simple action and add dimension to it by applying given circumstances.

Age: 8 plus.
Skills: Creating a character, focus, improvisation, mime and imagination.
Participants: This can be practised alone or in a group.
Time: 10–20 minutes.
You'll need: A room large enough for students to spread out and find a quiet space.
How to: The students find a space in the room and sit down on their own. The student imagines that they are packing a bag for an event; perhaps they are going on holiday, on a school trip, to school, to the gym, or travelling for a year, or even that they've been assigned to a spy mission. Explain that they can be any character they want, but they must know at least three of their given circumstances. For example, it's your first day at high school, you're in your tidy bedroom with everything neatly laid out on the sofa bed and you have stomach cramps. Or you are leaving home, you are in a rush because you don't want your parents to find out, you have a headache and your stuff is spread all over the room because you threw it all over the place in a rage.

Give the students a few minutes to mime packing their bags under a certain set of given circumstances and then ask them to try again with a brand-new set of circumstances. This can be done three or four times.

Variation: This exercise can also be done with a real bag and real objects. However, this can be distracting and too leading. If practised this way, explain the exercise the week before to students and ask them to bring in a bag and some objects. It can be good for students to swap their bags and objects with others so that the items they are using don't hold too many set connotations.

Tip: Students shouldn't rush this exercise or feel that they have to talk or *perform*. Subtle actions and reactions can be very intriguing, and these should come naturally if the student is playing the given circumstances.

The aim: A simple exercise where students learn how performing an action (packing a bag) can completely change depending on the given circumstances.

5.5 Entering the stage

An acting exercise created and taught by Uta Hagen to aid actors in delivering an authentic and believable entrance onto the stage.

Age: 8 plus.

Skills: Creating a character, focus, improvisation, charisma and imagination.

Participants: This can be practised alone or in a group.

Time: 10–20 minutes.

You'll need: A room with an area that can be used as a stage and an area that can be used as offstage.

How to: In Uta Hagen's book *Respect for Acting*, she talks about the problem many actors have of moving from backstage to onstage in a believable way. She notes that often actors either try and float onto the stage without being noticed or they enter the stage with a bang and an 'accept-me-or-else-dammit' attitude. Neither way is genuine or desirable. Hagen teaches that the actor should enter with purpose and focus and they should aim to be in, not on, the stage. She says the actor must prepare before going on stage by asking, 'What did I just do?', 'What am I doing right now?', 'What's the first thing I want?' (Hagen, *Respect for Acting*, p. 96).

First, the actor must know their given circumstances before they walk on stage and then they must know their first want. If they have a want that brings them on stage, this will make the entrance a lot easier. For example, maybe they are entering because they are looking for an object (a scarf perhaps), or they are looking for their coffee or checking the post. Giving the character a simple first want will help to make the entrance a lot more believable. Let's imagine that you are playing Ratty in *Wind in the Willows*. You're about to enter for your first scene where you meet Mole and go out on a boat together for a picnic. Just before your entrance, you should run through your given circumstances: it's a warm spring morning, the first warm day since last year. You slept well. You've prepared a beautiful picnic. You've been working on the boat for the last few weeks to make sure it's in good condition for its first sail day. Your first objective when you get onstage is to look for the picnic rug:

- Step one – (offstage) check the picnic basket for the rug and perhaps admire the delicious picnic you have put together.

- Step two – (offstage) close the picnic basket and consider where else the rug could be, concluding that you must have left it on the boat.

- Step three – (walking on stage) walk along the river bank towards the boat, hoping the picnic blanket is in there, noticing Mole on your way.

Then do this again, but try something different with the same entrance and character. For example:

- Step one – (offstage) open the picnic basket to admire the cupcakes you have made. You get tempted by the thick pink frosting and eat one.

- Step two – (offstage) adjust your waistcoat and while doing so notice that you've put on some weight this winter.

- Step three – (walking on stage) walk on stage, undoing your waistcoat, and head for the boat quickly as it's about time you were more active.

Then do this again, but try with a different entrance, character and circumstances. This doesn't have to be done with a character that's already been written. Original characters that spring from the imagination can be fun too. For example, you're coming home from school on a cold January day with a very heavy bag that's pulling down on your shoulders. You're standing outside your door and can't find your keys. Your mum won't be back from work for another hour. You've got basketball practice in 15 minutes and you have to get changed quickly and drop your bag off at home:

- Step one – (offstage) you take your heavy bag off your shoulders, cursing your teachers for making you carry heavy textbooks.

- Step two – (offstage) you search for your house keys in your bag and finally find them.

- Step three – (entering the stage) you open the door, enter the house with your heavy bag, throw down your keys and bag, and look for your basketball kit.

Give students about 10 minutes to practise several different ways of entering the stage with these guidelines. Then ask those who want to share to show it to the rest of the group and see if the class can guess the circumstances.

Tip: The students should practise this exercise with a character and scene that they already know well or that at the least has been explained well to them.

The aim: To help the actor enter the stage in character in a charismatic and believable way.

5.6 Improvising scenes from a character's past

An improvisation exercise to build upon the background material of a character.

Age: 8 plus.

Skills: Communicative skills, teamwork, creating a character, character building, improvisation and imagination.

Participants: This needs to be practised in groups of three or four.

Time: 10–20 minutes.

You'll need: A room large enough for students to rehearse in small groups.

How to: Split the students into groups of three or four. Explain that they are going to come up with a short scene from a character's past. If the students are working on a play, musical, monologue or scene in class, it's good to use one of the characters they are already playing. However, it can also be fun to do this exercise with a character from a fairy tale or book.

One person in each group will feature as the main character. So, for example, if the class is putting on a production of *Romeo and Juliet* and the actor playing Juliet is in the group, she might be a good choice. The students will create a scene from her past, for example, her ninth birthday party. The information devised does not have to be accurate or even as Shakespeare intended; students are free to create their own stories here. They must give the character at the centre of the scene their given circumstances. So perhaps Juliet is very wealthy, dressed in a beautiful white dress for her birthday and has been told to keep her dress clean. This can be the starting point for the improvisation. Given circumstances can be added for the other characters too. Perhaps her mother's given circumstances are that she's very wealthy, she's just had an argument with her husband, she feels the room is too hot and she's in a dress that is uncomfortably tight.

Students may be concerned about what is a given circumstance and what isn't; tell them not to worry and to relax as any information they add to their characters is good and can be used. The general rule, however, is that the given circumstances are the environmental and situational factors that influence a character's actions.

Tip: Try and be specific rather than general when possible. For example, instead of saying 'Juliet is wearing a dress', say, 'Juliet is wearing a white dress.'

The aim: For students to think about a character's past and to consider past given circumstances.

5.7 Conditioning forces

An advanced acting exercise where the actor adds several conditioning forces to the scene they are playing.

Age: 10 plus.

Skills: Concentration, improvisation, creating a character and spontaneity.

Participants: This can be practised alone or in a group.

Time: 10–20 minutes.

You'll need: A room with an area that can be used as a stage and an area for the rest of the class to sit and watch.

How to: Conditioning forces are something Uta Hagen talks about in her book, *Respect for Acting*. These are the conditions that influence a person's behaviour such as being in a hurry or in the dark, or being cold, hot, nauseous or hungry. The conditioning force may or may not be part of the given circumstances and it may or may not be in the stage directions. A good actor and director will add extra conditioning forces to a scene to bring it to life and make it more believable. Very often a character will be influenced by several conditioning forces at the same time, which can be a challenge for the actor. In this exercise, students practise performing up to five conditioning forces at once.

Ask a volunteer to come up onto the stage and explain that they are going to play the same scene several different times with different conditioning forces. The first conditioning force they are going to play with is time.

Ask the actor to imagine they are sitting at home at the kitchen table. They are eating breakfast and absorbed in something on the TV. They check the time and it's 8.05 am – time to leave for school. They turn off the television, get their school bag and coat, and leave for school determined they will not miss the bus.

1   Ask the actor to imagine they are sitting at home at the kitchen table. They are eating breakfast and absorbed in something on the TV. They check the time and it's 8.10 am. They might miss the bus. They grab their bag in a hurry, dropping some books, and have to pick them up, throwing them back in the bag. Totally disorganized, the actor grabs their coat, forgets their purse and has to dash back for it.

2   Ask the actor to imagine they are sitting at home at the kitchen table. They are eating breakfast and absorbed in something on the TV. They check the time and it's 8.15 am. They check again and can't believe it. They are going to miss the bus! They rush, trying to leave, totally disorganized, spilling their breakfast cereal and getting angry at themselves.

3   Explain to the students the ways in which a character's behaviour is very often influenced by time.

Now consider the second example where the character is in a hurry but not in a total panic. Ask the student to play this scene again, but add another conditioning force. Perhaps they have an ear ache, for example.

Then play it again but with three conditioning forces. Perhaps they are in a hurry, have an ear ache and it's a really hot humid day. Three conditioning forces are plenty for the beginner to work with. However, if you practise this exercise with a class several times over a number of classes, it's possible to add up to five conditioning forces. For five, perhaps the character is in a hurry, they have an ear ache, it's a hot humid day, they are nervous about some friendship issues they're having at school and they are wearing a new school skirt that is shorter than they would normally wear.

This exercise does not have to be practised with the actor leaving for school, although practising a situation where the character leaves for something works best. There are many made-up scenarios that can be used – leaving for a birthday party, leaving for a wedding or leaving for prom.

Variation one: Once the class has practised this exercise several times over a period of time, it can be fun to add another dimension – a lost object. So, for example, if the leaving for school example is used, the actor could play trying to find their homework, which is lost, with the conditioning forces on top of that. It can be really fun to have another student hide a piece of paper that the actor actually has to find while practising the conditioning forces.

Variation two: If students are working on a scene or show in class, explore how different conditioning forces can add dimension to this scene or a scene from the show.

Tip: As a class, before practising this exercise, come up with a long list together of different conditioning forces.

The aim: To encourage the actor to perform multidimensional and believable characters.

6 OBJECTIVES

Introduction

When an actor takes on a character, one of the first things they need to find out is their character's objectives. This includes all of the character's wants and needs, big and small. Objectives are not normally written into the script; instead, they tend to be added in by the director and/or actor. When the actor plays an objective, it adds subtext to the script.

There are two types of objectives: the objective and the super objective. The objective is the want in the scene or sentence. The super objective is the character's main want, their life ambition perhaps or their main want that drives the story. Examples of a super objective might include wanting to get married, to own a tapas bar, to get back from a space mission or to find one's father. In *The Wizard of Oz*, Dorothy's super objective is to get home to Kansas. But an actor may also like to add an unconscious super objective; for example, Dorothy might want to be accepted for who she is by her family. Super objectives can be conscious or unconscious, and the conscientious actor will work out both. Super objectives can create many of the smaller objectives. When Dorothy wants the gatekeeper to let her into the Emerald City, it's her objective to talk the gatekeeper into letting her in. This objective to get into the Emerald City is driven by her super objective to get home.

Characters often have needs too, which can be objectives or super objectives. Needs can be interesting as they can cause conflict for the character. For example, in *The Wizard of Oz*, when the Wicked Witch of the West casts a spell on the poppies, Dorothy needs to fall asleep, but her objective is to get to the Emerald City and her super objective is to get home. During this scene, the actress needs to play all three of these needs and objectives at once even though some of them conflict.

Nearly all actors, directors and writers spend a considerable amount of time thinking about a character's objectives, as it's these that bring a character to life and move the story forward. In this chapter, I outline several classical exercises and some fun warm-up games to encourage the actor to think about and play with the objectives of the character they are performing.

6.1 Why are you doing that?

A fun fast-paced group improvisation exercise where students take on an objective provided by another student.

Age: 10 plus.
Skills: Communicative skills, intuition, spontaneity, imagination and verbal reasoning.
Participants: This exercise needs to be practised in a group of five or more.
Time: 10–15 minutes.
You'll need: A space big enough for students to sit in a circle.
How to: Students sit in a circle, and one student – let's call her Li Jing – stands in the centre of the circle and starts doing something. Li Jing could be doing anything – cleaning, playing a guitar or practising magic tricks. Li Jing has to think of an objective as to why she is doing this activity. Maybe she is cleaning because her dad has said she can't go out until her bedroom is clean, she is practising the guitar because she wants to join a rock band or she is practising magic tricks because she wants to pass an exam at wizard school.

Someone else in the circle stands up and joins Li Jing; let's call him Harris. Harris asks Li Jing, 'What are you doing?' Li Jing carries on with what she is doing – let's say practising magic tricks – but replies with something completely different from what she is actually doing. Li Jing needs to say the activity and the objective. She might say, 'I'm giving my rabbit a bath because I'm taking him to a rabbit show', 'I'm practising gymnastics because one day I want to be in the Olympics' or 'I'm making a card to cheer up my best friend as she's upset about some bullies at school.' Harris will then start to do the activity with the objective that Li Jing just described.

After a few moments of Harris doing this action, the next person in the circle will come up and join him. That person will ask Harris, 'What are you doing?' Then Harris will give this person a new action and obstacle.
Tip: This game can seem confusing when the teacher explains it; the best thing to do is to practise and explain this exercise at the same time and then the students will pick it up quickly.
The aim: To encourage students to think fast and come up with an objective for a character without overthinking it.

6.2 Broken-down lift

A fun improvisation game where people with strong wants get stuck in a lift together.

Age: 10 plus.
Skills: Improvisation, intuition, spontaneity, imagination and creating a character.

Participants: This exercise needs to be practised in a group of four or more.

Time: 10–15 minutes.

You'll need: Some string to map out the outline of the lift on the floor.

How to: With a piece of string, mark out a square or rectangle that is about the size of the floor space in a medium to large lift. Ask four actors to volunteer for the improvisation and have the rest of the group sit and watch. Each of the actors thinks up an objective and a super objective for the character they will play in this improvisation. For example, it could be that you want to get to a job interview for an internship at a magazine (objective) and one day you would like to be the editor of that magazine (super objective). Note that the objective and super objective don't have to be linked. It could be you really want to get a coffee (objective) and it's your dream to one day find a cure for cancer (super objective). To make this game work its best to choose an objective that could be linked to taking the lift. Objectives for using the lift might include getting to work, to an interview, to the photocopying machine or to a photo shoot, or getting food, getting a coffee or going to the toilet. The super objective can be anything, and it doesn't have to be related to taking the lift.

Once the actors have their objectives and super objectives, they can get into the lift in character, and the improvisation begins. Explain that at some point in the improvisation, they need to imagine that the lift breaks down. Having four characters, each with an objective and a super objective, stuck in a lift together is a great premise for an improvisation. Enjoy!

Variation one: Instead of having the actors do the improvisation straight away in front of the class, the group can be split into groups of three or four and the actors can have 10 minutes to practise the lift improvisation before showing it to the rest of the group.

Variation two: This exercise can be practised in many different ways. It can be played without any objectives where students are given the freedom to improvise in any way they wish within the structure of the broken-down lift exercise. Or it can be played with the actors playing given circumstances (see the chapter on given circumstances) or with the actors playing an action each (see the chapter on actions). Advanced students can play the characters with given circumstances, an objective and an action.

Tip: Ask students to really imagine that they are in a lift and to think about how the confined space might affect their movement, speech and actions.

The aim: To show how objectives can build the tension and conflict within a scene and to help improve students' improvisation skills.

6.3 The telephone call

An improvisation exercise in which the actor makes a phone call to get something that they want.

Age: 8 plus.

Skills: Improvisation, intuition, spontaneity, imagination, persuasion and verbal reasoning.

Participants: This can be practised alone or in a group.

Time: 5–10 minutes.

You'll need: A phone on aeroplane mode to use as a prop.

How to: The actor can either do this on their own or in front of the class. The actor makes an imaginary phone call with a real phone with the objective of getting something that they want from the imaginary person on the other end of the line. Maybe the phone call is to a supermarket because they would really like a job there, to their friend because they would like their friend to come over and help them with their homework, or to Batman because they would like him to come and sort out a crime in the neighbourhood. Any idea is fine. Explain to the students that in order to make this exercise really effective, they should act out the listening as well as the speaking; acting is about listening, and it is often in those quiet moments when an actor listens that the best parts of the performance shine through. Of course the actor isn't really listening in this exercise, but they have to imagine that they are.

Variation: For advanced students, this can be played with the actors also playing given circumstances (see the chapter on given circumstances) or with the actor playing an action on the person on the other end of the phone (see the chapter on actions). For really advanced students, they can play the characters with given circumstances, an objective and an action.

Tip: The actor should try to imagine in their head exactly what the person on the other end of the phone is saying.

The aim: For the student to be able to hold an improvisation on their own, to act out listening and to play an objective throughout.

6.4 Group improvisation with objectives

In groups, students create a short improvisation where each character has a strong objective.

Age: 8 plus.

Skills: Improvisation, teamwork, creating a character and communicative skills.

Participants: This needs to be practised in groups of three or four.

Time: 20–25 minutes.

You'll need: A space big enough for students to rehearse.

How to: Ask the students to get into groups of three or four. Explain that they are going to create a 5-minute improvisation. In this improvisation, each character must have one want, and this want can be anything: to go to the moon, to have an ice cream, to be a world-famous skate boarder. Once each actor has thought up an objective; ask the group to agree on a setting for their improvisation. A public space works best, such as a park bench, doctor's waiting room, art gallery, airport or bus stop. Give the students about 10 minutes to practise an improvisation with those three or four characters together with their strong objectives in a public space. Once the 10 minutes is up, ask the students to show the improvisation to the rest of the class, and the audience can try and guess the characters' objectives.

Tip: Each actor should only play one objective. Simple objectives are acceptable; sometimes it's the simple ones that are the most effective. Something like 'wants to do their coat up (but the zip's broken)' is enough.

The aim: For students to create a group improvisation where objectives take centre stage and to show students that objectives are a great way to create conflict and action within a scene.

6.5 Objectives with props

A fun verbal reasoning exercise where students try to convince the group why they need an object the most.

Age: 8 plus.

Skills: Communicative skills, verbal reasoning, persuasion, lateral thinking and intuition.

Participants: For a group of five or more.

Time: 10–15 minutes.

You'll need: Anything between five and twenty props laid down in the centre of a circle of students. These props can be absolutely anything, but a variety is good. For example, a helmet, wooden spoon, scarf, mask, teddy bear, candle, coat, thermometer, headphones and yoga mat.

How to: The class sit in a circle, and in the centre of the circle, there is a collection of props. As explained above, this can be a collection of random objects. One student will then go to the centre of the circle, pick up one of these objects and explain to the circle of students around them why they really need that object. The person explaining needs to imagine that the class doesn't want them to have the object. The actor has to try really hard to talk the group into letting them have the object. For example, if Chen were in the centre of the circle and she picked up a doll, she would need to convince the class to let her have this doll. She can think of any made-up reason she likes. Perhaps she could explain that she really needs it for her little sister as her sister is in hospital and the doll will cheer her up. Or Chen might explain that this is her long-lost doll from childhood and she lost it on holiday when she was four. It's Chen's objective to make the class say yes she can have the object. Once Chen has finished her story, the class can respond with yes or no. Students can make the stories as elaborate as they like; if Chen were feeling adventurous, she could say the doll belongs to an enchanted empress and that if the class doesn't let Chen have it, she can take it back to the rightful owner and the empress will cast a terrible spell on the group!

Tip: Encourage students to make eye contact with the people in the circle as a means to get what they want.

The aim: For students to think laterally and improve their persuasion skills.

6.6 The objective/obstacle exercise

An acting exercise to introduce students to the idea of objectives and obstacles.

Age: 8 plus.

Skills: Communicative skills, intuition, listening, spontaneity, persuasion, imagination and verbal reasoning.

Participants: This exercise needs to be practised in pairs.

Time: 10–15 minutes.

You'll need: A space big enough for students to split up and work in pairs.

How to: Students get into pairs. One of the students in the pair – let's call her Bella – thinks of an objective. This can be anything; perhaps she's trying to talk a teacher out of giving her an after-school detention, she really wants her friend to go to a party with her or she really wants the circus master to take her on to train as a trapeze artist. The other student – let's call him Eugene – has to provide the obstacle. For example, if Bella wants to train at the circus, she may tell Eugen why she's the perfect person to train as a trapeze artist, but Eugen, playing the circus master, will find reasons not to take her on. Bella will need to try and change Eugen's mind. She may or may not succeed. The scene may go something like this:

Bella   Hi, excuse me, I watched your show last night. It was incredible. I …

Eugen   Thank you *(turns away)*.

Bella   I was wondering, do you have any training programmes or …

Eugen   Not at the moment.

Bella   Well, I've been doing gymnastics since I was like two and it's my dream to be a trapeze artist and I love your …

Eugen   I'm sorry, we're fully staffed.

Bella   I'd work really hard and I'd be happy to help out with other things while I train, selling popcorn …

Eugen   How old are you?

Bella   17, but I'll be 18 in August.

Eugen   You're too young.

Bella   But I'm really mature for my age, and people say I look 21. I can do the splits, a triple summersault, and my gymnastics teacher says ...

And the scene could carry on like that.

Once students have had about 5 minutes, ask them to swap over. Now Eugen will have an objective and Bella will provide the obstacle. If there's time, the class can sit down as an audience and watch some of these short improvisations.

Note of caution: It's important that the students are told not to make any upsetting or hurtful comments during the improvisation; for example, if Eugen said to Bella that she can't join the circus because she's too big, that would be inappropriate and potentially upsetting to Bella.

Variation: For students aged 13 years and older, it's possible to practise a memory version of this exercise. It's the same exercise, but students draw from a real-life experience in which they wanted something but someone was obstructing them. Bella will need to think of a time in her life when she really wanted something and then she will explain this story to Eugen in as much detail as possible. Perhaps she really wanted her mum to let her have a pet dog. Even though he is male, Eugen can still play her mother. Bella will tell Eugen the reasons her mum gave for not getting a puppy, explaining this memory to him in as much detail as possible. Eugen will play this character and scene, but it doesn't matter if he doesn't play this role perfectly; he just needs a general idea of how the scene went in real life and then he can play it how he wants after that. When Bella has given Eugen as much information as possible, she tries to remember the details of the room she was in, what she was wearing, how she was feeling and what else was going on in her life at that time.

Then Bella and Eugen can improvise this true scene. The hope is that the real feelings Bella had on that day start to emerge and she has an honest emotional response to the improvisation. It's not uncommon in this exercise for the student with the objective to become fully immersed in the improvisation and completely forget that they are in a drama class.

Note of caution: Like all memory exercises, this exercise should be practised with caution and only with older students. It can bring up an emotional experience and in some cases trauma. If, for example, Bella was asking her mum for a puppy because her previous dog had passed away, this may bring up all kinds of emotions for Bella. Explain that the improvisation can be stopped at any time. If trauma has been brought up during this exercise, ask the affected student to chat to you after class and check in that they are okay. If necessary, contact any caregivers whom the student has given you permission to contact. Before the exercise is practised, students need to be told not to choose a memory if someone in that scene has now passed away.

Tip: Physical force or contact should not be used in this exercise as a means for someone to get what they want or for obstructing someone for what they want. Only verbal reasoning should be used.

The aim: To show students how to put objectives and obstacles into practice.

6.7 Adding a need

An exercise where students take a scene and explore playing it with a hidden need.

Age: 8 plus.

Skills: Character building, literacy and imagination.

Participants: This needs to be practised in groups of two or more depending on the script.

Time: 25–30 minutes.

You'll need: A space big enough for students to rehearse and a short excerpt from a script.

How to: Designate each student a character and script and explain that they are going to act out the script but with a hidden need. For example, their character may need the toilet, to blow their nose or to do the washing up. Let's imagine students are working on the script below from *Romeo and Juliet*.

Romeo and Juliet

Written by William Shakespeare.

Cast: Lady Capulet, Nurse and Juliet

Juliet's mother and the nurse are telling Juliet what a fine marriage prospect Paris is. Juliet is not keen on the idea, but after some coaxing she says she will marry him if it will make them happy. This scene takes place before she meets Romeo.

Lady Capulet   Juliet! Juliet! Juliet!

Nurse comes running on out of breath.

Nurse, where's my daughter? Call her forth to me.

Nurse   I bade her come. God forbid! Juliet! Juliet!

Juliet   Madam, I am here. What is your will?

Lady Capulet sits Juliet down.

Lady Capulet   This is the matter. Nurse, give leave awhile,

We must talk in secret.

Nurse leaves.

Nurse, come back again;

Nurse comes back.

I have remembered me, thou's hear our counsel.

Thou know'st my daughter's of a pretty age.

Nurse   Faith, I can tell her age unto an hour.

Lady Capulet   She's not fourteen.

Nurse   Thou wast the prettiest babe that ever I nursed.

An I might live to see thee married once,

I have my wish.

Lady Capulet   Marry, that 'marry' is the very theme

I come to talk of. Tell me, daughter Juliet,

How stands your dispositions to be married?

Juliet   It is an honour that I dream not of.

Lady Capulet   Well, think of marriage now. By my count,

I was your mother much upon these years,

That you are now a maid. Thus, then, in brief:

The valiant Paris seeks you for his love.

Nurse   A man, young lady! Lady, such a man

As all the world – why, he's a man of wax.

Lady Capulet   Speak briefly, can you like of Paris' love?

Juliet   I'll look to like, if looking liking move;

But no more deep will I endart mine eye

Than your consent gives strength to make it fly.

For the actor playing Juliet, her need might be that she needs a glass of water, so she may be distracted looking around for a glass of water, and finally at the end of the scene, she gets one as the nurse hands it to her. A need for Lady Capulet could be that she needs to choose a dress for Juliet for the party that night. A need for the nurse could be that she needs to make the bed. Giving each character a need can add a dimension to the scene that brings it to life. Because the above scene is Shakespeare, make sure the students understand the text by chatting to them about it beforehand. Also explain to students that Shakespeare liked to have fun and that students can play with the text by making it modern. If they want to do that, perhaps Juliet's need throughout the scene is that she needs to reply to her friend's text message. Also tell them it's okay to have fun; perhaps the nurse's need is that she needs the toilet.

Variation: It's also possible to add a need to an improvisation exercise. Improvisation exercises which work well for this include 'I'm sorry I …' and 'I got you this present' (Chapter 4), 'Taxi driver with given circumstances' (Chapter 5), 'Broken-down lift' (Chapter 6), 'Hospital queue' and 'A job interview' (Chapter 7), and 'The letter', 'What are you doing?' and 'Park bench' (Chapter 8).

Tip: Basic needs work well – like needing some food, more sleep or a drink. Avoid making the needs too complicated.

Aim: For students to have fun and bring a character to life by adding a basic need.

6.8 Adding objectives to a scene

An advanced exercise where students take a scene and explore playing it with several different objectives to see how character motivations can change a scene.

Age: 8 plus.
Skills: Character building, literacy and imagination.
Participants: This needs to be practised in pairs.
Time: 25–30 minutes.
You'll need: A space big enough for students to rehearse and a short excerpt from a script.
How to (part one): Ask the students to get into pairs and give them a short duologue to work with. The example below from *Oliver Twist* is about the right length. Ask the students to read it through a few times and practise it, spending about 10 minutes on this.

Oliver Twist

Written by Charles Dickens, adapted by Samantha Marsden.

Cast: The Artful Dodger and Oliver

Oliver has almost reached London after walking for many days, when he meets the confident and playful Artful Dodger.

Dodger   Going to London?

Oliver   Yes.

Dodger   Got any lodgings?

Oliver   No.

Dodger puts his hands in his pockets and whistles, or hums if the actor can't whistle.

Oliver   Do you live in London?

Dodger   Yes. I do, when I'm at home. I suppose you want some place to sleep tonight, don't you?

Oliver   I do indeed, I have not slept under a roof for weeks.

Dodger   Don't fret your eyelids on that score. I've got to be in London tonight and I know a respectable old gentleman who lives there who will give you lodgings for nothing, and never ask for the change!

Oliver   Will he let me stay?

Dodger   Like I say, he'll give you lodgings for nothing, if someone he knows introduces you. And don't he know me? Oh boy he knows me! What's your name?

Oliver   Oliver.

Dodger pats Oliver on the back.

Dodger   Fagin's gonna love ya Oliver! Come on.

Dodger walks off and Oliver follows after him.

After the students are familiar with the text and they have had a chance to act it out, ask them to give the character they are playing an objective. Oliver, for example, could play a whole number of different objectives while performing the above scene. Ideas include:

- Wants to get away from the Artful Dodger.
- Wants to befriend the Artful Dodger.
- Wants to impress the Artful Dodger.
- Wants the apple the Artful Dodger is eating.

The actor chooses one objective and plays that. The same goes for the actor playing the Artful Dodger. The Artful Dodger could play this scene with a number of different objectives. Ideas include:

- Wants to recruit Oliver into Fagin's gang.
- Wants to leave the street quickly as he's just picked someone's pocket and he's afraid he might get caught by the police.
- Wants to know if Oliver has any money on him.
- Wants to hurry up and get back to Fagin's because he's hungry.

Once students have played this scene with one objective, ask them to do it again with a different objective, scrapping the first objective entirely and trying with a completely different one. This can be done three or four different times. Once this has been done, ask the students to choose the one objective each that worked best with the scene and then to practise this and show it to the rest of the class.

Part two: Once students are used to doing a scene with one short-term objective, they can move onto adding a super objective. Super objectives for Oliver might include:

- Wants a family.
- Wants to be loved.
- Wants to be safe.

Super objectives for the Artful Dodger might include:

- Wants to be rich.
- Wants to be a leader.
- Wants to be loved.

Ask the students to play the scene with the short-term objective they did in the first half of this exercise and to add a super objective.

Tip: Ask students to put themselves in the character's shoes and then to think about possible objectives that character might have.

The aim: To teach students how to apply work on objectives to the text.

7 ACTIONS

Introduction

The action refers to what a character does in order to achieve their objective. For example, if you'd like someone to lend you their prom dress, you might charm them, beg them or threaten them to give it to you. It is this charming, begging or threatening that is the action. Actions are an excellent means of creating subtext and they can bring a scene to life. An action word must always be a transitive verb or an active word (a doing word that reflects something you can actively do to someone else). I have provided a long list of actions in this chapter to help the student and teacher.

Below is a small example of adding actions to a script. The words in square brackets are the actions, but it should be remembered that actions are subjective and there are many ways to interpret this scene; this is just one example.

A Christmas Carol

By Charles Dickens, adapted by Samantha Marsden.

Nephew   [Animate] A merry Christmas Uncle!

Scrooge   [Dampen] Bah! Humbug!

Nephew   [Question] Christmas a humbug Uncle? You don't mean that I am sure.

Scrooge   [Dispirit] I do. Merry Christmas! What right have you to be merry? What reason? You're poor.

Nephew   [Challenge] What right have you to be miserable? [Accuse] You're rich.

Note that there doesn't have to be a new action for the start of every new sentence. New actions can be added at any point in the script; sometimes an action might be played for a few sentences and sometimes only for one word.

The actor can add an action to a physical movement as well as text. For example, if the actor puts a cup on the table, they could do this with an action to communicate an unspoken message to someone else in the room. The action might be intended to alarm, to pacify or to intimidate the other person. The action the actor, or the director, chooses will completely change the meaning being conveyed by putting the cup down on the table.

If a scene or monologue ever feels flat, adding actions is a good way to bring it to life. But it is important to know the characters' given circumstances and objectives before attempting to add actions to a character. Once this is known, the actor has the creative freedom to choose the actions that they think suit their character best. I have found that adding actions is a particularly useful tool for the young actor working on Shakespeare as this has a way of giving the text a clearer meaning and makes it quickly relatable.

Playing with actions is a wonderful technique for the rehearsal room, and it can bring a character and text to life; however, it should be noted that it is not a technique for everyone, and some actors may be able to instinctively play their actions without even realizing it. Sometimes writing actions down can bog down or block a performer, while in other cases it can help them. The good drama teacher should see which techniques work for different students and should use what works for the individual.

7.1 Shaking hands with actions

A fun warm-up where students shake hands and introduce themselves to one another while playing an action.

Age: 8 plus.
Skills: Social skills, improvisation and awareness.
Participants: This needs to be practised in a group of five or more.
Time: 5–10 minutes.
You'll need: A room big enough for students to stand in two long lines facing one another.
How to: Students get into pairs and stand opposite one another, forming two lines with about eight steps between them. One partner is named B and the other A. The teacher will call out an action for B and an action for A, and once this action is called out, the partners walk towards each other (playing the action), shake hands and introduce themselves. For example, the teacher may call out 'B – bully' and 'A – accept'. The students will then walk towards each other, B playing the action bully on A, and A playing the action accept on B. Once they reach each other, they shake hands and introduce themselves, both still playing

their action. With these given actions, there will be a whole fabric of subtext that the students will play without much prompting. Do this eight or nine times, changing the actions for both students each time. The list of actions in this chapter may be a useful resource for the teacher to draw on in this exercise.

Variation: Do the same as above, but instead of shaking hands, have the pairs do a different activity together, such as playing tennis, building a sandcastle or baking a cake. Call out the actions for them to perform while they play the chosen activity.

Tip: Start with simple actions everyone will be familiar with such as adore, bully, flatter and judge. Move onto harder actions later and explain the meaning of the word to the class. Harder actions might include pacify, repel, validate and lull. Explain to students that it's always okay to put their hand up to ask what a word means and that if they don't know the meaning of a word, chances are there are other people in the group who don't know either. No one should ever feel stupid for not knowing what a word means.

The aim: For students to learn just how much an action can change the subtext of a scene and the body language of a character.

7.2 Hospital queue with actions

A fun improvisation activity where a group of students all want an emergency appointment at the hospital. Each person has an action to play on the receptionist to try and get the appointment.

Age: 8 plus.
Skills: Social skills, improvisation and spontaneity.
Participants: This needs to be practised in a group of three or four.
Time: 10–20 minutes.
You'll need: A desk for the person playing the receptionist to sit behind.
How to: One person imagines they are a receptionist in an accident and emergency ward, and they sit behind a desk. Groups of three or four characters line up, all believing their case is urgent and that they have the right to skip the queue. Perhaps someone is in heavy labour, someone else is in agony with a broken leg and another person thinks they are about to stop breathing! Each person has to try and convince the receptionist that they should get to see the doctor first. Each of these people has one action that they play on the receptionist to try and get what they want. It's a good idea to give students a list of actions that they can choose from (a list is provided later on in this chapter). So, for example, the person in the late stages of labour might quiz the receptionist about giving her an appointment, saying things like, 'What's your policy for pregnant women?', 'What will your manger say when he finds me giving birth in this waiting room?', 'How long have you been working here?' and 'Do you even know what you're doing?' And let's say, for example, the person with the bad leg chooses

to accuse the receptionist; they might say things like, 'But you said it was only a 10-minute wait?', 'Do your systems even work?' and 'I think you're mistaken.'

Tip: Encourage students not to talk all at once; although their case is urgent, they need to listen to what others in the improvisation are saying too.

The aim: For students to have fun while improvising and seeing how actions can inflate conflict.

7.3 Improvising an advert with actions

A group improvisation activity where students put together an advert with an action directed at the audience.

Age: 8 plus.
Skills: Teamwork, improvisation, life skills, creativity and trust.
Participants: This needs to be practised in groups of four or five.
Time: 20–25 minutes.
You'll need: A space where students can rehearse.
How to: Students get into groups of four or five, and together they decide on a product to sell – maybe a shampoo, a computer or a new car. Now they decide on one action that they will try to make the audience feel, and then they create an advert around this. Say, for example, the group choose shampoo and enchant. They will then devise the advert so that it enchants the audience – perhaps with flicks of the hair accompanied by magical 'ahh' noises and a front on-camera commentary about the magical qualities of the shampoo. Or perhaps the group might choose to sell a new car and to shame the audience. They may make fun of an old model of car, saying things like, 'Are you too embarrassed to turn up to that party in your old car? Well, you should be. Impress your friends and family with our new ultra model!'

Once students have had about 15 minutes to practise this, ask them to show the advert to the other students, without giving away the action they are playing, and then ask the audience what they think the action was.

Variation one: Devising an advert as a team can also be done without playing an action and maybe more suitable for younger students.

Variation two: This exercise can be made into a bigger project where an advert is actually filmed. However, if filming students under the age of 18, the teacher will need written consent from the parents or guardians and the footage should not be shared on social media websites without the students' and parents' or guardians' consent.

Tip: Ask students to all agree on where the imaginary camera is. If the teacher has a camera, they can bring a video camera in and use it as a prop so that the students know where to focus their performance too. Note that students shouldn't be filmed without their parents' written consent.

The aim: For students to play an action as a team and to work as a team to create a devised piece with an action.

7.4 A job interview with actions

Students imagine that they are in a job interview with one playing the interviewer and the other the interviewee; both take on one action to play.

Age: 10 plus.
Skills: Social skills, improvisation, life skills and spontaneity.
Participants: This needs to be practised in pairs.
Time: 15–20 minutes.
You'll need: A desk and two chairs for each pair practising this exercise and a list of generic job interview questions – a list has been provided below.
How to (step one): Students get into pairs and take a sheet of paper with a list of job interview questions on it. Here's an example:

- Can you tell me about yourself?
- Why do you think this job is important?
- How would someone you know describe you?
- Why do you want to work for us?
- What experience do you have?
- What are your strengths?
- What are your weaknesses?
- Where would you like to be in your career 5 years from now?
- What did you like least about your last job?
- Can you give me an example of a time you went above and beyond the call of duty at work?
- Do you have any questions for us?

One person plays the interviewer and the other the interviewee, and they choose one action each. Perhaps the interviewer chooses to judge the interviewee and the interviewee chooses to charm the interviewer, thereby giving the interviewer the higher status. Or this could be turned on its head; perhaps the interviewer chooses to welcome the interviewee (perhaps they're desperate to fill the position) and the interviewee chooses to insult the interviewer. Ask the students to play this scene in several different ways to see how the action can completely change the dynamics of the scene and the relationship between the characters.

Step two: First, do the same as above, but for a more advanced exercise, ask the students to change the action several times throughout the scene. So perhaps the interviewer starts by welcoming the interviewee, but this changes during the course of the interview and they begin to belittle the interviewee. And likewise the interviewee can change their actions throughout, maybe starting by charming the interviewer but ending with begging them.

Tip: Know the job that the interview is for and the actions that will be played before the improvisation begins.

The aim: For students to use actions to help build characters and create meaning and subtext in an improvisation.

7.5 Changing the action

A fun fast-paced acting exercise to introduce students to playing with actions.

Age: 10 plus.

Skills: Communicative skills, intuition, listening, spontaneity, persuasion, imagination and verbal reasoning.

Participants: This exercise needs to be practised in pairs.

Time: 10–15 minutes.

You'll need: A space big enough for students to split up and work in pairs.

How to: Students get into pairs. One of the students in the pair – let's call him Aarav – thinks of an objective. This can be anything; perhaps he's trying to talk his mum into lending him her car, he really wants to return a phone he bought to the shop but he's lost the receipt, or he wants to get a job at a burger bar. The other student – let's call her Kay – has to provide the obstacle. For example, if Aarav wants to get a job at a burger bar, he may tell Kay why he's the perfect person to work there, but Kay will play the restaurant owner, saying there are no jobs available. Aarav will then need to try and change Kay's mind by using actions. He might start by trying to charm Kay, then he may change his action and try and excite her, and then he may change the action again and beg her. Once students have had about 5 minutes, ask them to swap over. Now Kay will have an objective that she tries to achieve with actions, and Aarav will be the obstacle. If there's time, the class can sit down as an audience and watch some of these short improvisations.

Variation: Practise the exercises as described above, but instead of the actors choosing the action, the teacher or a student calls out the action the actor is to play. So someone might call out, 'Aarav, thrill!' or 'Kay, snub!' and the actors perform the action called.

Tip: If students are new to actions, start off very slowly by adding just one or two actions to very short scene.

The aim: For students to play with actions and see how actions can change, or even lead, a scene.

7.6 Improvising with an action

A popular improvisation game where anything can happen but with the added dimension of playing actions.

Age: 10 plus.

Skills: Listening, spontaneity, imagination, verbal reasoning and improvisation.

Participants: This needs to be done in a group of five or more.

Time: 10–15 minutes.

You'll need: A room big enough for an audience and a stage space.

How to: Sit the class down as an audience and set up a space to be used as the stage. Ask two volunteers to step onto the stage. Let's imagine Bo and Prisha volunteer. They can improvise any scene they like. Explain that it's a good idea to know the location and what type of character they are and then to fully commit to this and improvise. The twist is that each actor will play one action. So Bo, for example, might choose the action to adore and Prisha may choose the action to belittle. Already you can have idea of where this improvisation may be going.

The pair on stage may improvise for 30 seconds or a few minutes. The two improvisers will freeze when someone in the audience claps their hands and shouts 'freeze!' The person who called out will now walk onto the stage and tap the person on the shoulder whom they want to leave. The person tapped will leave, and the new improviser will take the position they were frozen in. This new person will then join the improvisation by starting with a new idea and playing a new action; the person left on stage can change their action.

The exercise continues like this with audience members calling out 'freeze' when they would like to have a turn on stage. Explain to the students that if the two improvisers look like they're struggling, someone should call 'freeze' to help them or put them out of their misery! Also explain that if the improvisation is going very well, they should not call out 'freeze', and they should let everyone enjoy the magic that's being created on stage. It's also important to make it clear that no idea is too silly and all ideas are welcome. A nice touch to help students gain confidence is to encourage the audience to applaud each time a performer leaves the stage.

Variation: This exercise can be practised with a number of different improvisation exercises. Ones which work well for this include 'I'm sorry I …' and 'I got you this present' (Chapter 4), 'Taxi driver with given circumstances' (Chapter 5), 'Broken-down lift' (Chapter 6), 'Hospital queue' and 'A job interview' (Chapter 7), and 'Park bench' (Chapter 8).

Tip: Students should choose only one action, and this is the action they continue to play throughout the improvisation, no matter what happens. For students new to actions, the teacher can give lots of examples of actions so that students have something to choose from. There's a list of actions in this chapter which can be used.

The aim: For students to have fun and be creative by using actions in an improvisation setting.

7.7 Adding actions to a script

An exercise where students write the actions one line at a time onto their scripts.

Age: 10 plus.
Skills: Literacy, critical thinking, creating a character and analysis.
Participants: This needs to be practised in pairs.
Time: 20–30 minutes.
You'll need: A script and a pen for every student and a list of actions for every student.
How to (step one): First of all, explain to students that the action is the thing you do to obtain your objective. The action is powerful; it can sometimes speak louder than words, and different actions will change the meaning of a sentence. For example, if in the script the line is 'Would you like a drink?', this could be said in such a way as to welcome someone or to scare them. It's helpful to give students a list of actions to work with for this exercise. Below is an introductory list:

Accept	Destroy
Accuse	Disappoint
Adore	Educate
Advise	Electrify
Aggrieve	Enchant
Aid	Enrage
Amuse	Examine
Annoy	Expose
Badger	Flatter
Beg	Force
Bewitch	Guide
Bribe	Hearten
Bully	Henpeck
Calm	Hush
Challenge	Ignite
Confront	Indulge
Confuse	Inform
Console	Insult
Convince	Irritate
Crack	Isolate
Dazzle	Jolly
Deflate	Judge
Defy	Lull
Delay	Madden

Misdirect	Relieve
Mistreat	Repel
Mother	Rescue
Nag	Sadden
Obey	Serve
Obstruct	Shame
Offend	Silence
Outshine	Support
Pacify	Teach
Pamper	Tease
Pardon	Tempt
Persuade	Terrify
Pester	Thank
Petrify	Tolerate
Praise	Trigger
Prepare	Upset
Provoke	Urge
Punish	Validate
Quiz	Weaken
Refuse	Welcome
Reject	Worship

Once students have had a look at a list of actions and they have added any they might want, hand out a short scene for them to work on. This can be any scene. Once they have the scene, ask them to write on it, adding one action to each line. Below is an example with the actions in brackets. However, please bear in mind that actions are a subjective choice and those outlined below are just one interpretation.

Jane Eyre

Written by Charlotte Brontë, adapted by Samantha Marsden.

Cast: Hannah and Jane

Jane has run away from her rich fiancé, Mr Rochester, at the altar as she found out he already had a wife. She has been walking in the rain for days and feels as if she's about to die. She knocks on a stranger's door for help.

Hannah *(opens the door and is surprised to see Jane)*   [Judge] What do you want?

Jane   [Coax] May I speak to your mistress?

Hannah [Reduce] Why? Where do you come from? Who are you?

Jane [Deflect] I am a stranger.

Hannah [Judge] What is your business at this hour?

Jane [Sweeten] I want a night's shelter in an out-house or anywhere, and a morsel of bread to eat.

Hannah [Pity] I'll give you a piece of bread, but we can't take in a beggar to lodge.

Jane [Engage] Please let me speak to your mistress.

Hannah [Belittle] No. You should not be out at this hour, it does not stand you in good stead.

Jane [Beg] But where shall I go if you send me away? What shall I do?

Hannah [Shame] Oh, I'll wager you know where to go and what to do. Here's a penny; now go.

Jane [Urge] A penny cannot feed me, I have no strength to go farther. Don't shut the door. Oh don't for God's sake!

Hannah [Diminish] I must; the rain is driving in.

Jane [Command] Tell the mistress of the house, let me see her.

Hannah [Disappoint] Indeed, I will not. You are not what you ought to be, or you wouldn't make such a noise. Move off!

Jane [Plead] But I will die if I am turned away.

Hannah [Attack] No, you may have plans to rob this house. You may have followers, housebreakers.

Once the students have entered their actions, ask them to act out the scene with these actions in mind. Then ask them to do it again but this time with different actions, writing the new one just above the previous one perhaps (a messy rehearsal script is an actor's prerogative). Explain that all the best actors play and experiment and that it's possible to try this scene in dozens of different ways until they find the interpretation that works best. Once they've found the best interpretation, hand them a fresh copy of the script, which they can write their chosen actions onto.

Step two: Instead of students writing in the action at the beginning of each sentence, have them write it anywhere they like in the text. Here's an example:

Hannah (*opens the door and is surprised to see Jane*) [Judge] What do you want?

Jane [Coax] May I speak to your mistress?

Hannah [Reduce] Why? [Belittle] Where do you come from? Who are you?

Jane [Still coaxing] I am a stranger.

Hannah [Judge] What is your business [Belittle] at this hour?

Jane [Sweeten] I want a night's shelter in an out-house or anywhere, [Beg] and a morsel of bread to eat.

Hannah [Pity] I'll give you a piece of bread, [Dampen] but we can't take in a beggar to lodge.

Jane [Engage] Please let me speak to your mistress.

Hannah [Shame] No. You should not be out at this hour, it does not stand you in good stead.

Jane [Plead] But where shall I go if you send me away? What shall I do?

Hannah [Shame] Oh, I'll wager you know where to go and what to do. [Hurry] Here's a penny; now go.

Jane [Urge] A penny cannot feed me, I have no strength to go farther. [Attack] Don't shut the door. Oh don't for God's sake!

Hannah [Diminish] I must; the rain is driving in.

Jane [Command] Tell the mistress of the house, let me see her.

Hannah [Disappoint] Indeed, I will not. You are not what you ought to be, or you wouldn't make such a noise. [Attack] Move off!

Jane [Plead] But I will die if I am turned away.

Hannah [Attack] No, you may have plans to rob this house. [Shame] You may have followers, housebreakers.

Tip: This exercise works best when the students already know the play and characters: they can choose actions that suit the character's personality.

The aim: For students to learn how actions can change a scene, and to encourage students to experiment with actions.

8 IMAGINATION

Introduction

Audition panels are not looking for actors who can imitate; they are looking for actors who can create, and it's the imagination which inspires us to create characters that are unique. There are thousands of different ways to play Lady Macbeth, for example, and it's our imagination that allows us to create our own interpretation. In order to create, we need an active and well-exercised imagination, which is why so many actors continue to train and take classes even after they've 'made it'.

Konstantin Stanislavsky famously says that 'art is a product of imagination', and in his seminal book, *An Actor Prepares*, he dedicates a whole chapter to the imagination. It's here that he introduces us to the 'magic if'. With the 'magic if', the actor puts themselves into the character's shoes and asks, 'What would *I* do if I were in this situation?'

While practising the exercises in this chapter, the actor should not force the imagination; instead, it should be coaxed and encouraged. Ideas should never be dismissed, even if they seem crazy or even terrible! The actor needs to try each exercise without judgement, and the teacher needs to hold back judgement too. It's important that both student and teacher don't over analyse and critique every performance in the classroom as the actor needs to silence the inner critic. Failure should be encouraged as sometimes good ideas come out of bad, and very often we only arrive at the good ideas by going through the bad ones. The imagination lives in the subconscious, and the subconscious can be very shy, particularly in public. We need to praise it like a timid child. When I teach I often say, 'Don't think, just do!' This is my way of saying, 'It's okay to act from the subconscious.'

The imagination is activated by activity. Therefore, in this chapter, I provide activities to wake up the imagination and give it a full workout.

8.1 The letter

An entertaining improvisation exercise that teaches the participants to trust the imagination and follow their instinct.

Age: 8 plus.
Skills: Imagination, improvisation, storytelling and spontaneity.
Participants: This exercise can be done alone or in a group.
Time: 10–15 minutes.
You'll need: One blank piece of paper folded in half. The group sits as an audience facing a lone actor on the stage.
How to: Take a blank piece of paper, put it in a blank envelope and lay it on the floor.

The actor walks in, opens the envelope and reacts to what's inside. Perhaps in the letter, there are bad exam results, or the letter is from an enemy making a threat, or it's from Hogwarts with an invite to wizard school.

If a large class is doing this exercise, it can be fun to sit everybody down as an audience, watching the actor open the letter, as the adrenaline of having an audience can propel the imagination.

Variation: It's also possible to do this exercise with added circumstances. Perhaps, for example, the character about to open the letter has a bad back, the house is freezing and they can't afford any heating. Or, it could be that it's the character's first day at university, there's a heat wave and they got very little sleep the night before. If a group is practising this exercise, it can be fun to have the audience provide the circumstances to the actor.
Tip: The actor may want to plan what's in the letter and choose an idea before they get up on stage, or they may want to be spontaneous and go with the first idea that comes into their head while they open the letter on stage. Either way is fine; every student is different and they should exercise their imagination in the way they feel most comfortable with.
The aim: To teach the actor to trust their imagination and then to fully commit to that idea, no matter how wacky!

8.2 Imagine you are ...

A fast-paced and simple imagination exercise good for warming up a group.

Age: 8 plus.
Skills: Imagination, confidence, improvisation, listening, energy and spontaneity.
Participants: This exercise can be done alone or in a group.
Time: 5–10 minutes.
You'll need: A space large enough for the group to move about in. Ask the students to find a space on their own in the room.

This exercise encourages the imagination to act on imagined stimuli. The teacher, or a student, calls out an action that stimulates one of the five senses (taste, smell, touch, sight and hearing). The students then act upon that instruction. Examples include:

- Imagine you are looking at the world's tallest skyscraper (sight)
- Imagine you are eating a slice of sweet moist carrot cake (taste)
- Imagine you are stroking a long-haired cat (touch)
- Imagine you can hear the sea on a stormy day (hearing)
- Imagine you can smell a public swimming pool (smell)

After each instruction, give the group a minute or two to imagine the sensory experience and to act out.

Tip: Being specific helps with this exercise. Instead of saying, 'Imagine you can hear music', it would be better to say 'Imagine you can hear a really loud rock band.'

The aim: To warm the group up and to encourage spontaneity.

8.3 What are you doing?

A high energy improvisation game taken from Konstantin Stanislavsky's *An Actor Prepares*.

Age: 8 plus.

Skills: Communicative skills, imagination, confidence, improvisation, listening, energy, spontaneity and trust.

Participants: Pairs.

Time: 10–15 minutes.

You'll need: The group to stand together in pairs in their own space within the room.

Background: In Stanislavsky's *An Actor Prepares*, there is a conversation between Stanislavsky and his director, Tortsov. Stanislavsky is frustrated by the failure of his imagination, and Tortsov tells him this is because

in the first place, you forced your imagination, instead of coaxing it. Then, you tried to think without having an interesting subject. Your third mistake was that your thoughts were passive. Activity in the imagination is of upmost importance. (Tortsov in Stanislavsky, *An Actor Prepares*)

The director then goes on to play a game with Stanislavsky to illustrate his point. Below is a slightly adapted version of this exercise.

How to: Two actors stand, or sit, facing each other. Label one actor A and the other B. A does a simple action, for example, drinking tea from an imaginary cup.

B asks, 'What are you doing?'

A replies, 'I am drinking.'

B then comes up with a new circumstance that provokes a reaction; this must be related to the activity A chooses. For example, B might say, 'What if it were vinegar in that cup?'

A reacts as if there is vinegar in the cup.

After recovering from drinking vinegar, A performs another simple action. For example, A could sit down.

B asks, 'What are you doing?'

A replies, 'I'm sitting down.'

B replies proactively with a new circumstance; perhaps, 'What if you were sitting on an ant nest?'

A reacts as if sitting on an ant nest.

And the exercise continues like this. After a few minutes, A and B should swap over so that both partners get to experience both sides of the activity.

Tip: Explain to students that it's important that they react to each other and that they accept all ideas without hesitation.

The aim: To encourage the participant to react to their own and their partner's imagination. The exercise encourages play and listening skills.

8.4 Let me tell you a story about ...

A storytelling game where students create a story based on an object.

Age: 8 plus.

Skills: Communicative skills, imagination, confidence, improvisation, listening and storytelling.

Participants: Pairs.

Time: 10–15 minutes.

You'll need: Anything between five and twenty props laid out in the centre of a circle of students. These props can be anything, but variety is good. Examples include a hair dryer, a mug, a pair of shoes, a toy car, a pen, a wig, an apple, keys, a book and some soap.

How to: The class sit in a circle, and in the centre of the circle, there's a pile of props. As explained above, this can be a collection of any random objects. One student then comes into the centre of the circle, takes one of these objects and tells the class a made-up story about the object. The more eccentric the story, the better! If Alex picked up a bar of soap, he could tell the class any story he liked about it. Perhaps he would explain that it is a magic bar of soap that makes you invisible as you lather it into your skin. He might go on to tell a story about how he once used the invisible soap at school and then he sneaked into the staff room and found out that all the teachers were aliens! Or he might tell a different story about how it's a very old soap that his granddad had during the war and how his grandfather never used the rose-scented soap because the smell reminded him of his granny; instead, when he was in the trenches, he would sniff it to remember her.

Variation: Split the class into groups of four or five, and give each group an object. Give them 10 minutes to create a short improvisation based on that object. Once these scenes have been devised, they can be shown to the rest of the class.

Tip: Encourage students to use eye contact and to use their pauses while telling their stories about the object.

The aim: For students to build the confidence and skills to create and tell stories.

8.5 Park bench

A fun improvisation exercise to help participants react intuitively and think fast.

Age: 8 plus.
Skills: Imagination, confidence, improvisation, listening, energy, spontaneity, social skills and trust.
Participants: Pair work to be performed in front of a group.
Time: 10–15 minutes.
You'll need: A bench or three chairs put together in the shape of a bench. The group sits facing the two actors on the bench.
How to: One person sits on the park bench and does a simple action; for example, they could eat sushi, drink coffee or do a crossword puzzle. Another person joins the original person on the bench. It is the new person's aim to get the first person to leave the bench but without using any physical force. Perhaps the new person could be very annoying; maybe they pick lice out of their pet dog's fur, or they talk about how the world will end soon, or they won't stop talking about how they're going to win the next *X Factor* while doing demonstrations of their audition. The actors should react to each other's imaginations without blocking one another. If one actor starts to block the other, the exercise should be stopped and started again.
Variation one: It's also possible to do this exercise with actions (see Chapter 7, Actions). For example, it could be one character's action to *terrify* the other character, and it could be the other character's action to *thank* the first character. There is a long list of actions to draw from in Chapter 7.
Variation two: This exercise can be done with given circumstances. For this the student needs to know the who, when, where and why for their character. For example, it could be one character's given circumstance that she's a manager of a large firm, it's her lunch break, she's in the park and she is on her laptop to prepare for the meeting. The other person's given circumstances could be: she's a teenage girl, it's her lunch break and she's in the park hiding because she's told a terrible lie about her best friend and has just been found out.

Variation three: This exercise can also be done with objectives. For this each person sat on the bench would play one objective. For example, maybe one of the people might want to finish reading his newspaper and the other person might want to borrow some money for a bus fare.

Variation four: The advanced actor can try playing the character's given circumstances, actions and objectives all at the same time within the framework of the park bench exercise.

Tip: *Park bench* is a highly versatile acting exercise which can be played in a number of different ways. Start with the simple version and build in variations slowly.

The aim: To encourage participants to react to their fellow actors in a spontaneous way.

8.6 If I were a …

A low energy creative exercise to encourage actors to imagine what it's like to be someone, or something, else.

Age: 8 plus.

Skills: Teamwork, creativity, listening, spontaneity, storytelling, character building and focus.

Participants: This exercise can be done alone, but it's better to practise it as a large group.

Time: 5–10 minutes.

You'll need: The group to sit on the floor, or on chairs, in a circle.

How to: One person starts this exercise by saying, 'If I were a … ', then they fill in the blank with a person, animal or thing; for example, a politician, a snail, a sunflower. The next step is to add a want for this person, animal or thing. For example, 'If I were a politician, I would want some smart shoes.'

If a lone actor is practising this exercise, they can list more wants for this character verbally, or they can write them down. For example, the politician may also want a husband, a garden, some lunch, a promotion and a cause to believe in.

If this exercise is being done as a group, I suggest the group sit in a circle and create the character's wish list as a team. So the person starting might say, 'If I were a prince, I would want a palace of my own.'

The person next to them might add, 'A sword'.

Then the next person in the circle might add, 'Some privacy'.

Continue going around the circle with each person saying the first imagined want for the prince that comes to mind. It may go like this:

'If I were a prince, I would want a palace of my own.'

'A kingdom'.

'A horse'.

'A princess'.

'A private jet'.

'To be normal'.

Once everyone in the circle has contributed a want, try again with a new character. For example:

'If I were a teacup, I'd want a saucer.'

'A peppermint teabag'.

'A clean cupboard'.

'Some super glue'.

'A dishwasher'.

'A careful owner'.

'A draught'.

'A soft washing-up brush'.

It's important that during this exercise no one is made to feel silly for the idea they've contributed. There are no right or wrong answers when it comes to developing characters, and all ideas should be accepted.

Variation: After the group has created a wants list, one actor can become the character. The actor sits on a chair in the centre of the circle, in character, and answers questions from the group.

Tip: Imagine what this person, animal or thing would want, not what *you* would want.

The aim: Encourages students to imagine what it's like to be someone else and to learn that different characters have different objectives.

8.7 Story circle

A group exercise in which students create a story together using everyone's ideas.

Age: 8 plus.

Skills: Imagination, improvisation, storytelling, listening, teamwork and spontaneity.

Participants: This exercise has to be practised in a group.

Time: 10–15 minutes.

You'll need: The students sitting in a circle.

How to: Students sit in a circle, and each student in turn will say one sentence as part of a story. For example:

Student one: Once there was a lonely witch.

Student two: Who liked to eat frogs.

Student three: And she liked to listen to opera music.

Student four: But one day she met a frog who sang opera.

Student five: So she didn't eat it; instead, she tried to make friends with it.

And the exercise continues like this.

It's very important that a student can say 'pass' if they want to; no one should ever be forced to contribute. Forcing a student into creativity can put them off for life – they must always have the option to pass. In my experience if you don't force students, you'll find that by week three or four, every single student will volunteer to participate. For this exercise, explain that no idea is ever too 'silly' and that all ideas are welcome. However, remind students that it's good for the story to have a protagonist (a leading character) and some conflict.

Variation: Another way to play this game is to have students say just one word at a time. For example:

Student one: A
Student two: long
Student three: time
Student four: ago
Student five: a
Student six: girl
Student seven: found
Student eight: a
Student nine: magic
Student ten: potato.

Tip: If students are struggling for ideas, explain that it's okay to draw on stories they already know for inspiration.

The aim: To encourage students to listen to each other, to trust their imaginations and to be spontaneous.

8.8 The magic box

An imaginative exercise where students mime, pulling objects out of an imaginary box.

Age: 8 plus.
Skills: Imagination, mime and focus.
Participants: This exercise can be practised alone or in a group.
Time: 10–15 minutes.
You'll need: A space big enough for students to sit in a circle.
How to: The students sit in a circle and the teacher goes to fetch a magic box. To really up the drama, it's fun if the teacher physically leaves the room and comes back in, miming carrying a very heavy box. The teacher sits in the circle with the students and carefully places the box in front of them. The teacher explains that this is a magic box and inside there are many different kinds of wondrous objects. In the past all sorts of things have been pulled out of it: tennis rackets, hamsters, apples, sweets, magic wands and cars, and once there was even a tiger in there! The teacher should really ham this up to get everyone

in the imaginative spirit! Then the teacher can open the lid and mime taking something out of the box. The person miming can use their body, face and voice to express what they have found and they can sit down, stand up, run around the room and do whatever they feel is right. However, the person miming must not say what the object or living thing is. After they've had 30 seconds to a minute to perform their mime, they can put the thing back into the box, close the lid and ask the audience to guess what it was. Then the box can be passed to the next person. Encourage students to imagine that the box is really there and to mime picking it up, putting it down, closing the lid and opening the lid.

Tip: Ask students to think about how heavy their object is, what the texture is like, if the object moves and, if so, how fast it moves.

The aim: For students to express their imaginings and ideas through mime.

8.9 Pass the object

A fun warm-up game to wake up the imagination.

Age: 8 plus.
Skills: Imagination, energy, mime and confidence.
Participants: For a group of five or more.
Time: 10–15 minutes.
You'll need: One prop to pass around the circle. Props that work well include a tennis racket, a scarf or a pen.
How to: The teacher takes one object – let's imagine it's a pen – and holds it up to the class, explaining that this is not any old pen but a magic pen! This pen can transform into absolutely anything. Then the teacher starts demonstrating how it can be a toothbrush, a golf club or even a baby being rocked in their arms. Then they explain that the pen will be passed around the circle and that when it reaches a student, they can turn it into anything they like. Nothing is too silly. But they must not tell the group what they have turned it into. If anyone doesn't want to participate, they may pass the pen onto the next person without doing the mime.
Tip: Encourage students to give the audience as many physical clues as possible as to what they have transformed the object into.
The aim: For students to use their imagination in relation to objects.

8.10 The five senses

An exercise to awaken the imagination and improve awareness.

Age: 8 plus.
Skills: Concentration, creativity, improvisation, focus and awareness.

Participants: This exercise can be done alone or in a group.

Time: 10–15 minutes.

You'll need: A relaxed group and a large space for them to move around in.

How to: It's best to start this exercise with a relaxation exercise from Chapter 1. Once the actor is relaxed, they should lie on the floor (if they are not already) and close their eyes. While the students are lying down, the teacher asks them to imagine themselves in a particular place. The place should be somewhere with plenty of sensory stimuli. Examples include a cave, the beach, a fun fair, the North Pole, the supermarket, an enchanted castle, up in the clouds, etc. Let's go with a cave for now. The teacher asks the students to imagine that they are standing in the cave. The teacher then poses questions as the students remain lying down with their eyes closed. The questions must all be related to the five senses. Below are some examples:

- Sight: What can you see? What's the ground like? What colour are the cave walls? Are there any marks on the walls? How big is the cave? Can you see the entrance? How much light is there, and where is it coming from? Can you see bats? Spider webs? How high is the roof?

- Hearing: What can you hear? Can you hear anything in the cave? Or outside the cave? Is there a waterfall nearby that you can hear? Can you hear the rustling of insects? What does it sound like when you move, and is this followed by an echo?

- Taste: What can you taste? Do you have something in your bag that you could eat? If yes, eat it: what does it taste like? Is it sweet? Savoury? Do you like it? Are you hungry?

- Touch: What can you feel? What's the ground like under your feet? Hard? Soft? Dusty? Slippery? What happens if you touch the floor? Do you get dirt on your fingers? What does that feel like? Can you touch the cave wall? Is it warm? Cold? Rough? Smooth?

- Smell: What can you smell? Does the cave smell of bat droppings? Or does the air smell fresh? Can you smell that someone has lit a fire in here recently? Can you smell your lunch on your breath? If you sniff the floor, what does it smell like?

Spend time on questions in the same vein as the ones above. Don't rush this exercise. Once the teacher has finished the questions, the students can open their eyes, stand up and explore the cave at their own pace. They can walk around it, touch it, sit in it, lie in it, smell it and do whatever else they like. The aim is to awaken all of the five senses in this imaginary situation. Once the exercise comes to an end, students should lie down again and spend a few minutes bringing their five senses back to the environment of the classroom.

Variation: This exercise can also be practised with music in the background to help stimulate the imagination.

Tip: It's best if the teacher uses a calm and neutral voice when posing questions during this exercise.

The aim: To awaken the imagination with the five senses and inspire students to be mindful while performing.

8.11 The 'magic if'

A creative exercise used to build believable characters based on Stanislavsky's 'magic if'.

Age: 8 plus.

Skills: Empathy, social skills, imagination, spontaneity and character building.

Participants: This exercise can be done alone or in a group.

Time: 10–15 minutes.

You'll need: Warmed-up participants and a large space for them to move around in.

Background: The 'magic if' is part of Stanislavsky's 'system' for training actors, and it is used to open up the actor's imagination. Stanislavsky thought that the actor should constantly ask, 'What would I do if I were in this character's position?' Stanislavsky didn't believe the actor could fully become another character but instead that the actor must understand all the given circumstances, and then ask themselves, considering such circumstances, 'What would I do if … '

It is the actor's job to believe in the 'magic if'. Children tend to find this easier than adults. I find 4- to 6-year-olds to be the best actors I work with, and sadly from about the age of 7, the ability to 'make believe' starts to fade; for many the ability has gone entirely by the time they reach their twenties. Part of the actor's job is to have the imaginative flexibility of a 5-year-old. To achieve this, the actor must play, accept all ideas that spring into the imagination and not be inhibited by what others think.

How to: This is a simple improvisation game to keep the imagination healthy. For this activity, the students should respond as themselves, and not as a character, and they should dive into the action without any reservations. The teacher, or student, calls out scenarios that begin with, 'What if … ' and then the students react. Below are some examples:

- What if you lost your dog?
- What if you were waiting for the school bus?
- What if you were at a school disco?
- What if you were at Disney World?

The exercise can be done alone or with many students spaced out around the room with the teacher calling out the 'What if … '

Variation: This exercise can also be practised with given circumstances. Here are some examples:

- What if you are a businesswoman, or man, dressed in an expensive suit, it's raining and you've lost your dog in the park?
- What if it's your first day at day at school, you have a cold and you're waiting for the school bus?
- What if you've just been crowned prom king or queen, your shoes are causing blisters on your feet and you're still at the school prom?
- What if you are a Mickey Mouse fanatic in fancy dress at Disney World?

Tip: Encourage students to move around the space in anyway they feel is right for the 'magic if'. They can sit down, walk, run, mime and even use props if they have them to hand. There should be no limitations, and students should be encouraged not to copy one another but to act from their own impulses.

The aim: To work the imagination and introduce students to Stanislavsky's concept of the 'magic if'.

8.12 The smell exercise

This is an advanced exercise drawn from method acting and used by many professional actors. Practise with caution.

Age: 11 plus.
Skills: Concentration, imagination, focus and awareness.
Participants: This exercise can be done alone or in a group.
Time: 10–20 minutes.
You'll need: The group to be relaxed and comfortable with one another. Ask them to find a space in the room on their own.
A note of caution: Method actors use memories to stimulate the imagination. This can be dangerous as some memories can be traumatic and distressing. Affective memory exercises seek memories from emotionally turbulent times and should not be attempted by students under the age of 18. For this reason, affective memory exercises have not been included in this book. However, I have included this smell exercise, taken from method acting, which uses memory recall to stimulate the imagination.

Although this is a method acting exercise, it is not an affective memory exercise. Many actors use smell memory on set to quickly access emotions, and I have found it to work well with my students under the age of 18. However, this exercise should be practised with caution. Don't use smells that could trigger upsetting memories. The smell of a hospital or a church, for example, could be risky memories to trigger, so it's best to avoid them. Remembering something like the smell of fresh baking bread is much safer – although, of course, there is still a possibility of trigging distress with this if somebody once had a traumatic experience while smelling baking bread. If the student starts to have a worrying response to the recall of a smell, the actor should stop the exercise immediately and focus on the breath, breathing in and out, deeply and slowly.

How to: In preparation for this exercise, it is good to do a relaxation exercise from Chapter 1. Once the actor is relaxed, they should find a private space in the room. Sitting down, standing up, lying down or walking around the room are all suitable options.

The aim of this exercise is for the actor to remember a smell and then to respond authentically to that smell without forcing a reaction. The teacher will call out smells and the actor will recall a time they smelt the smell. The memory should happen first and then the reaction. If the actor cannot remember the smell, or if they've never smelt it, it's fine for them not to react. Or they may need to sit and wait for a minute or two while they try and remember the smell. This exercise is not about an external performance; it is about triggering the imagination with a memory. Below are some examples of smells that could be used in this exercise:

- Baking bread
- A steam train
- A pet shop
- A freshly painted room
- The dump
- A new book

Spend 2 to 3 minutes on each smell, allowing the memory of the smell to affect the students. Students can be still or move around the room in response to the smell, whatever they feel most comfortable with.

Once the exercise has finished, it is good for students to reflect on how the smells affected their movements and emotions. If this was practised as a group, talking about the experience with others works well. However, no one should share their experience if they don't want to.

Variation: Give the students a short monologue to work with; pick two monologues – one for a female to play and one for a male to play. Let's take Juliet's well-known monologue from *Romeo and Juliet* as an example.

Romeo and Juliet

Written by William Shakespeare.

The clock struck nine when I did send the Nurse.
In half an hour she promised to return.

Perchance she cannot meet him. That's not so.
Oh, she is lame! Love's heralds should be thoughts,
Which ten times faster glide than the sun's beams,
Driving back shadows over louring hills.
Therefore do nimble-pinioned doves draw love
And therefore hath the wind-swift Cupid wings.
Now is the sun upon the highmost hill
Of this day's journey, and from nine till twelve
Is three long hours, yet she is not come.
Had she affections and warm youthful blood,
She would be as swift in motion as a ball.
My words would bandy her to my sweet love,
And his to me.
But old folks, many feign as they were dead,
Unwieldy, slow, heavy, and pale as lead.

In this monologue Juliet is newly in love and feeling frustrated with the nurse for taking so long to get a message to Romeo. Ask students to remember a time that they felt frustrated and to try and remember any smells that they can associate with that. Also ask them to try and remember a time they felt in love and any smell they can associate with that. Allow them some time to recall the smells and then ask them to perform the monologue.

Tip: Try using the smell exercise with scripts and monologues that the students know well.

The aim: To connect the actor to a real-life experience and then for the truth of that experience to shine through in their performance.

8.13 Imaginary objects

An advanced and highly focused acting exercise taught by Lee Strasberg.

Age: 11 plus.
Skills: Concentration, creativity, improvisation, focus and awareness.
Participants: This exercise can be done alone or in a group.
Time: 15–20 minutes.
You'll need: A relaxed group, spread around the room in their own space.
Background: The famous acting coach Lee Strasberg, often referred to as the father of method acting, believed in the power of concentration to spark the imagination. He came up with the concept of 'creative concentration'. Strasberg believed the actor must develop their concentration in order to bring fiction alive with the mind. He developed the 'imaginary object exercise' as a means to achieve this.

How to: Before doing this exercise, it is important to do a deep and long relaxation exercise. The aim of this exercise is for the actor to really believe in the existence of an imaginary object. This exercise can be done with any object, although sensory objects work best, for example, a cup of hot coffee, a plate of spaghetti or a scented rose. Strasberg famously uses a cup of coffee in his description; however, many under-18s won't be able to relate to this, so let's use a cup of hot chocolate for now.

The actor should sit on a chair and imagine a table and cup of hot chocolate in front of them. They should try to see the materials the table and cup are made of, the shape of both objects, the size and the distance they are from the actor. Then, slowly, the actor can reach for the cup and pick it up, remaining very slow and aware, mindful of the feel of the handle, the weight of the cup, the heat coming from it. Is there cream on the hot chocolate? Marshmallows? The actor should be aware of the hand holding the cup, making sure the hand is in the right shape to fit a cup into it. Now the actor can bring the imaginary cup towards them, imagining how the hot drink might move within the cup. This should be done very slowly and gently. Is the cup too hot on the hand? Or does it feel like it's the right temperature to drink?

The actor should now try to smell the hot chocolate. It's at this point in the exercise that the actor should scan the body for any tension and notice if they find any, still holding the cup. The actor can now bring the drink to their lips. They can try to feel the heat on their lips and smell the intensifying aroma. The actor should not worry about their facial expressions or what they look like. The concentration should be 100 per cent on the object. Now the actor brings the rim of the cup to their lips, perhaps licking the rim of the cup to see what it feels like on the tongue. Now very slowly the actor can taste the drink. Is it sweet or creamy? Warm or hot? Can the actor feel it going down the throat? Then, in their own time, the actor can finish the drink.

Tip: Explain to students that this is not a performance and that it doesn't matter whether or not it looks like they are drinking a cup of hot chocolate. It is the experience of feeling like they are holding a cup of hot chocolate that matters.

The aim: The aim is for the actor to have a truthful experience with the imagined object.

9 PHYSICALIZING CHARACTERS

Introduction

Body language is often the primary mode of communication between people, even more so than spoken language. It's often body language that reveals the subtext, given circumstances, objectives and actions of a person. Body language between people can also expose their relationship with one another, who has the higher status and whether or not they like each other. Many actors, writers and directors are obsessed with body language as it's the way subtext, character and story are communicated to an audience. One exercise all actors should do on a regular basis is to sit in a public space and watch people's body language, looking out for little gestures and physical quirks that can be used for future characters.

A well-prepared actor will understand their characters inside out, their given circumstances, objectives and actions, and they will also have a good grasp of how people communicate through body language. After all of this preparation and training, the hope is that the appropriate body language will come naturally in the performance. Body language should not be forced; it should come from a place of feeling and research. The performance will feel unauthentic if the actor says to themselves on stage, 'My character is feeling defensive so I'll cross my arms.' Ideally, the physicalization of a character should come naturally after all of the preparation.

In this chapter, I have provided some exercises for students to play with physicalization so they can experiment with body language and its effects.

9.1 Pairs

A warm-up game to encourage students to think about the stories they can communicate through freeze frames.

Age: 8 plus.
Skills: Communicative skills, imagination, mime and energy.
Participants: This exercise is practised in pairs.

Time: 5–10 minutes.

You'll need: A device to play music on and some fairly upbeat music.

How to: Ask the students to get into pairs and play some music that the pairs then walk around the room to. When the music stops, the teacher calls out a phrase that provides the inspiration for the pairs to create a freeze frame: for example, king and queen, Romeo and Juliet, night and day, happy and sad, cat and dog, or employer and employee. Explain to the students that they need to use their whole bodies and faces to create the image and that it's better to be over the top than to not go for it enough. Once everyone is in their freeze frame, the teacher can pick out an interesting one and ask the whole class to gather round and take a look at it.

Variation: This exercise can also be practised with individuals with just one thing being called out; for example, monkey, warrior or apple. Or it can be practised in larger groups of three or four; in this case, locations work well, for example, beach, chocolate factory or the moon.

Theming: The variation part of this exercise can be themed. Let's imagine that you are leading a jungle workshop. In this case, the game could be played as above in the variation section, but the teacher calls out only jungle-themed words, for example, snake, gorilla, explorer or banana tree. The students then freeze into these positions.

Tip: While walking around the room, encourage students to use up all of the space and to change direction and to be aware of how others are walking around the room, but not to copy.

The aim: For students to use their bodies to communicate stories.

9.2 Changing the tempo

A fun warm-up game where students explore the different speeds people operate at.

Age: 8 plus.

Skills: Creating a character, imagination and movement.

Participants: This exercise can be done alone or in a group.

Time: 5–15 minutes.

You'll need: A room big enough for students to walk around in.

How to: Students find a space in the room, and the teacher explains how different people move at different speeds. Ask the students to think of someone they know who moves around at top speed and someone they know who moves around very slowly. Now explain that they are going to move around the room at different speeds, which will vary depending on what number the teacher calls out. If the teacher calls out number one, students will move at a very slow speed, and if the number ten is called out, they will move at a fast pace. Students then add a character inspired by the speed. If number two is called out, for example, a suitable character might be a person who is at ease on holiday at the beach or a person who isn't very enthusiastic about going somewhere. Then, if the number eight is called, the actor might walk around the room fast as if they are late for a meeting or excited on their way to the gates at Disney World. Running isn't allowed in this exercise, even when the number ten is called; a fast walk is the maximum speed allowed. The teacher calls out all the different numbers, asking students to come up with characters and situations for each number.

Ask the students to choose their favourite character and speed from the ones they just experimented with. Some students may choose a slow character, number one or two, and others may choose a fast one, nine or ten. Ask the students to walk around the room as their chosen character. Instantly, the diversity of speeds will create an interesting scene and annoyances, and conflicts emerge as people get in each other's way.

Variation one: Ask the students to get into pairs; within the pair, one will play a low-speed person and the other a high-speed person, but despite this they both have the same objective. Perhaps they are looking for a lost dog, trying to complete a school assessment or trying to tidy a room. Conflict will arise in this scene because they are playing opposite tempos, and it's quite likely some comedy will spring from this.

Variation two: The characters created in this exercise can also be used in a number of improvisation exercises. Improvisation exercises which work well for this include: 'I'm sorry I …' and 'I got you this present' (Chapter 4), 'Taxi driver with given circumstances' (Chapter 5), 'Broken-down lift' (Chapter 6), 'Hospital queue' and 'A job interview' (Chapter 7), and 'Park bench' (Chapter 8).

Tip: Explain to students not just to focus on the speed of which a character walks but also to consider the speed of their body language. Someone at a number ten, for example, might have very rapid and frequent body language.

The aim: To show students that a person's natural speed/tempo affects the body language and dynamics of a scene.

9.3 Physical habits

A playful exercise where students add physical habits to characters to bring them to life.

Age: 8 plus.
Skills: Creating a character, creativity, movement and awareness.
Participants: This exercise can be done alone or in a group.
Time: 10–15 minutes.
You'll need: Explain to students the week before practising this exercise that for homework they need to watch everyone around them for physical habits. This can include friends, family, people on television, the general public – anyone

and everyone. The teacher should warn students not to vocalize their findings to those being observed, or to people who know them, as that could hurt people's feelings! Ask the students to write down the physical habits that they find, keeping the people who were observed anonymous. This might include all kinds of things such as twiddling with hair, chewing a thumbnail or blinking hard.

On the day of the exercise, the teacher will need a large piece of paper and a thick pen, a short duologue script for everyone in the class (example below) and a space big enough to rehearse in.

How to: Once the students have had a week to observe people's physical habits, ask them to sit down and share their findings with the class. Explain to the students that they should not name any of the people they observed as there is the potential here for people's feelings to get hurt. The teacher, or a volunteer student, can write everyone's observations down on a large piece of paper so that everyone can see them. Here's an example of what the list might look like:

- Scrunching the nose up
- Pushing spectacles up the arch of the nose
- Pulling on an earlobe
- Running the tongue along the upper teeth
- Pushing cuticles back
- Blinking frequently
- Plating hair
- Leaning in while someone talks
- Chewing the bottom lip
- Taking a long, deep, loud breath
- Tapping
- Stroking an eyebrow
- Taking a ring on and off
- Showing the palms of the hands in submission
- Fiddling with a watch strap
- Brushing T-shirt down
- Gesturing with the hands while talking.

After the group has created a long list, hand out a scene for students to work on. For this exercise, it's important that students have a strong idea of who the characters are in the scripted scene. Therefore, the piece will need to be a scene and story the teacher is familiar with and can explain to the class.

Let's imagine the class are going to work on a scene from *The Secret Garden* by Francis Hodgson Burnett. This is a story about two children, Mary and Colin, who are pessimistic, unhappy and seemingly set in their ways, but in the course of the story, they change for the better through their joint love of a secret garden they discover.

After providing some background information on the story, hand out the scenes, pair people up and ask the students to choose a character and give them just one physical habit. This can either be a physical habit from the list the class created together or a new one. But it should just be one. Encourage students to think about the physical habit they have chosen; it should be something that reflects the character. Let's imagine the students are working on the script below.

The Secret Garden

Written by Frances Hodgson Burnett, adapted by Samantha Marsden.

Cast: Colin and Mary

Colin is lying in bed; he believes he is very ill. He has become friends with Mary. But Colin is very jealous of Mary's other friend Dickon.

Colin   Why didn't you come to my room?

Mary   I was working in the garden with Dickon.

Colin   I won't let that boy come here again if you go with him instead of coming to talk to me.

Mary   If you send Dickon away, I'll never come into this room again.

Colin   You'll have to if I want you.

Mary   I won't.

Colin   I'll make you. They shall drag you in.

Mary   Shall they? They may drag me in, but they can't make me talk when they get me here. I'll sit and clench my teeth and never tell you one thing. I won't even look at you. I'll stare at the floor.

Colin   You are a selfish thing!

Mary   Selfish people always say that. You're more selfish than I am. You're the most selfish boy I ever saw!

Colin   I am not! I'm not as selfish as your fine Dickon is! He keeps you all to himself when he knows I am all by myself. He's selfish!

Mary   He's nicer than any other boy that ever lived! He's like an angel.

Colin   An angel? But he's a common cottage boy off the moor!

Mary   He's better than a common rajah! He's a thousand times better!

Colin lies down in his bed and turns over away from her.

Colin   I'm not as selfish as you, because I'm always ill and I'm going to die.

Mary *(really angry)*   You're not!

Colin *(sits up really angry)*   I'm not? I am! You know I am.

Mary   I don't believe it! You just say so to make people sorry.

Colin   Get out of my room! *(He throws his pillow at her.)*

Mary   I'm going and I won't come back.

One of the most creative parts of being an actor is choosing the interpretation of the person you're playing. If you are playing Mary in this scene and you are choosing a physical habit for her, there is no right or wrong so long as you have a reason for making that choice. The actor may choose pulling on an earlobe as her physical habit; perhaps this could be a reflection of Mary missing her mum because one of the last things her mother said to her was that she could get her ears pierced. Or the actor may choose to straighten down her hair each time Mary feels insecure because in the past other children teased her for her frizzy hair. What's important for this exercise is that the student chooses one physical habit, thinks up a reason for it and then implements this habit throughout the scene. It should be noted that the actor shouldn't overdo the habit; if it only appears twice in the scene that may be enough, although the actor may choose to do it more frequently if they feel that's right for the character. Once students have had some time to rehearse this scene with the physical habit, they can show it to the rest of the class.

Tip: Keep the physical habits subtle and don't overplay them.

The aim: For students to become more observant of others and to really think about the backstories that may provoke a physical habit.

9.4 Fairy-tale mime

An exercise where students tell a fairy tale through mime.

Age: 8 plus.
Skills: Teamwork, movement, mime, group awareness and concentration.
Participants: This exercise needs to be practised in groups of three or more.
Time: 25–30 minutes.

You'll need: A piece of instrumental music that is 2 to 3 minutes long; it should be an emotive but simple piece that can underscore a fairy tale.

How to: Ask the students to spilt into groups of three, four or five and explain that in these teams they are going to tell a fairy tale in 2 to 3 minutes using only mime. Any fairy tale is fine; ideas may include *The Ugly Duckling, Little Red Riding Hood, Cinderella* and *Sleeping Beauty*. Ask the students to first choose their fairy tale and then the character they will play and then ask them to lie down and close their eyes. Now play the piece of music that they will perform their fairy tale to. Make sure the music is instrumental; a classical or film soundtrack piece will work well. While students are lying down and listening to the music, hopefully their imaginations will run wild with ideas of how they are going to perform this fairy tale.

Once the music has been played, give the students 15 to 20 minutes to practise their piece together, playing the music on repeat so they can add the movement to it. Explain that the best mimes will be simple and work with the music. Not every scene from the fairy tale needs to be included; instead, encourage students to choose only the most important scenes in the story to perform. Less material and more polished is better than covering too much of the story and rushing the piece. Once students have rehearsed, ask them to show their mimes accompanied by the music to the class.

Variation one: Instead of students miming the fairy tale, the teacher can ask them to come up with eight tableaux that tell the story. Then they can rehearse these eight tableaux and run them in order, holding each for 6 seconds. This can be performed with music for dramatic effect.

Variation Two: For students studying a text, this exercise can be done with students creating eight important tableaux from the play and performed as in variation one. If the students know the play very well, they can do the first part of this exercise, miming the important scenes from the play to music.

Tip: Simplicity is key. Explain to students that simple actions done well are much more effective than lots of actions done half-heartedly.

The aim: For students to communicate stories through only their faces and bodies.

9.5 Exploring how props and costume affect movement

An exercise where students allow clothing and props to affect their movement.

Age: 8 plus.
Skills: Creating a character, imagination, movement and awareness.
Participants: This exercise can be practised alone or in a group.
Time: 10–15 minutes.

You'll need: A piece of costume or a prop for every person in the class. Things that work well include hats, gloves, scarves, coats, shoes, feather boas, walking sticks, sports equipment and bags.

How to: Ask each student to choose one piece of costume or a prop from the pile. Once they have the item, ask them to find a space in the room, to sit down with their object and to really imagine what type of character might wear or use this object. Once they have imagined that character, ask them to slowly start to move as that character, either putting the piece of costume on or holding the prop. Now students can move around the room as that character, considering how the character interacts with the item. A confident hockey player, for example, may hold their hockey stick with pride as they march to hockey practice. Or someone with low self-esteem may have a beloved scarf that they like to hide behind, pulling it right up over their chin and lips as they walk around the room hunched into their scarf. Ask the students to imagine what else their character might wear and own and how those things may affect the character's movement.

Once students have let this object or piece of costume affect the physicalization of a character, ask them to put the items back into the centre of the room and to choose a different item so they can try the exercise again, this time creating a new character with a new item.

Variation one: After students have experimented with three or four different items, ask them to put them all back in the centre of the room and to sit down as the audience. Students who want to can now show the rest of the group the character they have created by being hot-seated. The actor will pick up their item, sit on the hot seat chair in character and answer questions from the audience.

Variation two: The characters created in this exercise can also be used in a number of improvisation exercises. Improvisation exercises which work well for this include: 'I'm sorry I …' and 'I got you this present' (Chapter 4), 'Taxi driver with given circumstances' (Chapter 5), 'Broken-down lift' (Chapter 6), 'Hospital queue' and 'A job interview' (Chapter 7), and 'Park bench' (Chapter 8).

Tip: Ask students to consider what their character's relationship is with the object. Is the hockey stick one lent to them by their school or one handed down to them from their granddad, for example?

The aim: For students to allow costumes and props to affect the physicalization of a character.

9.6 Playing with eye contact

An exercise where students explore how eye contact can change the physicality of a character, the relationship between characters and the meaning of the scene.

Age: 8 plus.
Skills: Communication skills, character building, life skills and movement.
Participants: This exercise needs to be practised in pairs.

Time: 15–20 minutes.

You'll need: A short duologue and for students to be familiar with the scene.

How to: Give students a duologue, preferably the week before so they can familiarize themselves with it at home. Once students have had a chance to run the scene several times with their partners, get them to name one of themselves A and the other B. Let's imagine that they are working on the script below.

Pride and Prejudice

Written by Jane Austen, adapted by Samantha Marsden.

Cast: Lizzy and Jane

Jane and Lizzy are sisters. Their story takes place in the late eighteenth century, a time when women of a certain class and age were preoccupied with who they would marry. Jane is excited as she thinks she has found someone who is well suited to her. Lizzy is cynical about the likelihood of finding someone suitable whom she can also love.

Jane *(very excited)*   Mr Bingley is just what a young man ought to be. Sensible, good humoured, lively and so much at ease.

Lizzy *(not impressed)*   He is also handsome.

Jane   I was very flattered when he asked me to dance a second time. I did not expect such a compliment.

Lizzy   Did you not? I did. But that is one of the great differences between us. Compliments always take you by surprise, and *me* never. Of course he would ask you to dance again. You were about five times as pretty as every other woman in that room. Well, he certainly is very agreeable. You have liked many a stupider man.

Jane   Lizzy!

Lizzy   Oh, you like people too easily you know. You never see a fault in anybody. All the world is good and agreeable in your eyes. I've never heard you speak ill of a human being in your life.

Jane   I always say what I think.

Lizzy   I know you do; it's that which makes me wonder! You're clever, but you never see the foolishness of others. You look at the good of everybody's character and still make it better. You say nothing bad. Did you like his sisters? Did you not find them rude?

Jane   I was not sure of them at first, but after I spoke with them I found them pleasing. They are to live with their brother. I think I will become great friends with them.

Lizzy looks unconvinced.

Using the above script, go through the following exercises. Step one – person A is playing Jane and person B is playing Lizzy. Ask A (Jane) to try and make eye contact with B (Lizzy) throughout the scene, but Lizzy doesn't reciprocate. Step two – now change this to the other way round so that person B (Lizzy) tries to make eye contact, but person A (Jane) doesn't. Step three – neither A nor B make eye contact. Step four – both A and B make eye contact. Step five – students choose the eye contact combination they think works best for the scene. This can be done with many different scenes so long as there isn't a large status gap between the two characters.

Variation: This exercise can also be done without a script. Ask the students to get into pairs. Name one in the pair A and the other B. A will start by being a person with high status and B will be someone with low status. For example, A might be a queen and B a servant. Or A could be someone interviewing people for a job and B an interviewee. It is important to note that a job title doesn't necessarily give someone higher status. For example, A could play the higher status as a student and B the lower status as a teacher, perhaps because it's the teacher's first day at school and B is a student testing the teacher's boundaries. Ask A to try and make eye contact with B, but for B to avoid eye contact with A. Ask the students to come up with a 1- or 2-minute improvisation where A has higher status than B and A is trying to make eye contact, but B has lower status and is trying to avoid eye contact.

Now ask the partners to swap over so that B has a turn at being the person with the higher status who tries to maintain eye contact and A the lower status person who tries to avoid eye contact.

Once the pairs have both had a turn at playing with both statuses, ask them to choose the improvisation they thought worked best, and then ask them to practise once more and then show these to the rest of the class.

Tip: Give students the script a week or two before this exercise is practised and explain that the more they are familiar with the script, the easier it will be to do this exercise. In an ideal world, the students would learn the script off by heart, but that's not entirely necessary.

The aim: For students to learn the impact eye contact can have on a scene.

9.7 Adding tension to create character

An exercise where students add tension to the body to create a character through physicalization.

Age: 8 plus.
Skills: Creating a character, awareness and movement.
Participants: This exercise can be done alone or in a group.
Time: 15–20 minutes.

You'll need: The students to do one of the exercises from Chapter 1, 'Relaxation and Focus', before practising this exercise and a space students can move around in.

How to: First, get the students to relax by doing one of the relaxation exercises from Chapter 1. Then, once students have cleared their bodies of tension and are as neutral as possible, ask them to walk slowly around the room. Ask them to become very aware of their bodies and if there is in any tension to release that tension. The students should be aiming for a neutral walk free from tension and mannerisms. Now ask the students to add tension to one part of their body or face and to walk around maintaining that tension. The shoulders might be a good place to begin. There's no need to overact this and for students to instantly lift their shoulders up to their ears; the imagined tension can be subtle. The actor walks around with tension in the shoulders and imagines a character who has tension in this part of the body. Perhaps the character is someone who works at a computer all day. If so what does this character do at the computer: accounts, testing video games or something else? After a few minutes of creating this character, ask the students to shake it out and walk around in a neutral position again. Now add tension to another part of the body, perhaps the jaw, lips, neck, fists, forehead, hips or eyebrows. If it's the jaw, for example, then ask why this character holds tension there; is it because they are frustrated with life? Or are they someone who feels they have to keep quiet when really they want to speak out. Once some experimenting has happened, ask the students to shake it out, walk in neutral and then try another place of tension.

Variation one: It can be fun to add a tension to a character. Hand out a short scene and ask students to apply one tension to one part of the body for the character they are playing. If the below script from Lewis Carroll's *Alice in Wonderland* were used, the person playing Alice, for example, may want to play her with the tension in the hands. The person playing the hatter could play him with tension in the shoulders. The person playing the hare could play him with tension in the lips. And the person playing the dormouse could play him with tension in the nose. These are just examples; it's up to the actor to decide where or if they play any tension in the body.

Alice in Wonderland

Written by Lewis Carroll, adapted by Samantha Marsden.

Hare and Hatter   No room, no room!

Alice   There is room!

Hare   Have some lemonade ... Oh, there isn't any! *(Laughs)*

Alice   Then it wasn't very polite of you to offer it.

Hare   It wasn't very polite of you to sit down without being invited.

Hatter   Your hair wants cutting.

Alice   You shouldn't make personal remarks. It's very rude.

Hatter   Why is a raven like a writing-desk?

Alice   I believe I can guess that.

Hare   Do you mean that you think you can find out the answer to it?

Alice   Yes.

Hare   Then you should say what you mean.

Alice   I do! At least I mean what I say. That's the same thing you know.

Hatter   Not the same thing a bit! You might as well say that I see what I eat is the same thing as I eat what I see.

Hare   You might as well say I like what I get is the same as I get what I like.

Dormouse *(in his sleep)*   You might as well say that I breathe when I sleep is the same as I sleep when I breathe!

Hatter   It is the same thing with you. *(Silence)*

Hatter   What day of the month is it?

Alice   The fourth.

Hatter *(looks at his pocket watch)*   Two days wrong! *(Angry at Hare)* I told you butter wouldn't suit the works.

Hare   It was the best butter. *(Mumbles)*

Hatter   Yes, but some crumbs must have got in as well, you shouldn't have put it in with the bread knife.

Hatter takes a look at his watch and dips it into his tea.

Hare   It was the best butter you know.

Hatter   The dormouse is asleep again. *(He pours some tea onto the dormouse waking him up.)* Have you guessed the riddle yet?

Alice   No, have you got the answer?

Hatter I haven't the slightest idea!

Hare Nor I.

Hatter *(sings)* Twinkle, twinkle, little bat! How I wonder what you're at! Up above the world you flylike a tea tray in the sky.

Twinkle, twinkle …

Dormouse *(in his sleep)* Twinkle, twinkle, twinkle …

Ask students to show the scene to the class and the audience can guess where each actor chooses to place the tension.

Variation two: It's possible to add tension to a character in an improvisation exercise to help create a character or to bring a character a life. Improvisation exercises which work well for this include: 'I'm sorry I …' and 'I got you this present …' (Chapter 4), 'Taxi driver with given circumstances' (Chapter 5), 'Broken-down lift' (Chapter 6), 'Hospital queue' and 'A job interview' (Chapter 7), and 'The letter', 'What are you doing?' and 'Park bench' (Chapter 8).

Tip: When adding a tension to the body, encourage students to isolate that area and to try to only allow that one area to become tense. This can take some practice!

The aim: To show students that people are rarely neutral and free of tension and that when an actor plays a character, they should think about where that character holds the tension and why.

9.8 Body language for an interview

A fun exercise where students learn some of the messages body language can communicate.

Age: 8 plus.

Skills: Communication skills, character building, self-awareness, life skills, social skills and movement.

Participants: This exercise needs to be practised in pairs.

Time: 15–20 minutes.

You'll need: A table and two chairs set up as if there's going to be a job interview, a list of job interview questions for the person playing the interviewer and a list of body language gestures and their meanings.

How to: Ask the students to get into pairs. Ideally, the pairs should each have a table and two chairs set up in the style of an interview, but if there are not enough tables for everyone, just two chairs with an imaginary table in the centre will be suitable. Explain that one person will play the interviewer and the other will play the interviewee. This can be for any job the students like; they can decide this between themselves. Hand out a list of questions to the person who will be conducting the interview. Here's an example:

- So can you tell me about yourself?
- Why do you think this job is important?
- How would someone you know describe you?
- Why do you want to work for us?
- What experience do you have?
- What are your strengths?
- What are your weaknesses?
- Where would you like to be in your career 5 years from now?
- What did you like least about your last job?
- Can you give me an example of a time you went above and beyond the call of duty at work?
- Do you have any questions for us?

Ask the students to create two characters and to act out a job interview using the above questions. They can pick any job and character that they like.

Now ask the students to do this again, but this time ask both the interviewer and interviewee to add one piece of body language from the list below.

- Crossing arms – defensive
- Rubbing the palms together – expecting something positive
- Shoulder shrug – submissive
- Pouting the lips – desire
- Scratching head – uncertain
- Hand-to-face gesture where the index finger points up the cheek and the middle finger covers the mouth – thinking critical thoughts
- Head and chin down – doesn't want to be there
- Sucking in the lips – keeping quiet while thinking negative thoughts
- Hands in pockets – doesn't want to talk
- Palms down on the table – conveying authority
- Hugging self – scared
- Hands to heart – desire to be accepted
- Finger pointing – authoritative
- Fiddling with clothing – insecure

- Open arms – open to ideas
- Bringing the closed fist to the mouth – lying or holding back information
- Scratching the nose – can be a sign of lying
- Open palms – honest and open
- Biting the lip – anxiety
- Twirling hair – flirting
- Nail biting – nervous
- Rubbing the thumb and finger together – thinking about money
- Fist clenched – frustration
- Fingertips touch one another but palms don't (the steeple) – confident

Now ask the students to do this again but this time choosing a different piece of body language from the list. Once students have done the job interview in two different ways, ask them to swap over so that both students get a chance at being the interviewer and interviewee. Then, once all the experimenting is over, ask some students to perform the interview and then instigate a group discussion about how body language affects the interview.

Tip: Ask the students to consider how much the character they are playing wants the job and how that affects their body language.

The aim: To show students the power of body language and to have them experiment with it so that in a future job interview they can have more control over how they come across.

9.9 Takeaway words

An advanced acting exercise where the actor performs a monologue without using words. This is particularly useful for those preparing a monologue for an audition.

Age: 11 plus.
Skills: Reflective thinking, creating a character, literacy and awareness.
Participants: This exercise can be practised alone or in a group.
Time: 25–30 minutes.
You'll need: The student to know a monologue off by heart.
How to: The actor will need to know a monologue very well in order to do this exercise. The actor finds a space in the room on their own and spends a few moments getting into character, thinking of their character's given circumstances, objectives and actions. Then they perform the monologue with no words, but this does not mean they are miming the words. The actor should think through the monologue in their head, rather than speaking it. As they do so, they act it out using their face and body. The actor should be careful not to

overact, and the physical acting should be kept believable; the content of the monologue should be expressed through body language and facial expressions.

Variation one: The above exercise can also be practised by a pair working on a duologue or group who are working on a scene. However, the whole cast will have to know the piece very well in order for it to work.

Tip: To be able to practise this exercise, the actor will need to know the script off by heart.

The aim: For the actor to learn how to communicate a character's internal thoughts through the movement of the body and face.

10 CREATING A BELIEVABLE PERFORMANCE

Introduction

Creating a believable performance is hard. The actor has to know and perform all of the complexities and contradictions within their character and then deliver this in an authentic way while never forcing it. A convincing actor will perform at an internal level as well as an external one, playing with how a character presents themselves and what's actually going on inside. When the actor portrays both the character's internal and external dimensions, a three-dimensional or even a multidimensional character blossoms. Humans are complex, and there are often many thoughts, conflicts, contradictions, motivations and needs going on underneath the surface; when all of these workings are played, a believable character emerges. This is the actor's ultimate pursuit.

One problem I often come across, particularly with teenage actors, is that they try too hard to project their performance outwards while avoiding an internal performance at all costs. My guess is that they fear looking vulnerable. But in order to be an actor, a person must show vulnerability. It is those who are brave enough to perform from a place of vulnerability and truth that tend to gain the places at the top drama schools. To aid with this, the drama teacher needs to first of all create a safe space for the students to rehearse in, then they need to do all the ground work (relaxation, voice, movement, given circumstances, objectives and actions), and then, finally, the teacher should encourage vulnerability and truth. After all of this work, the student will hopefully be equipped and brave enough to perform a believable character in front of a theatre audience or film crew.

10.1 Sitting on a chair with purpose

An exercise Konstantin Stanislavsky practices in *An Actor Prepares*, where the actor learns how to 'sit on a chair'.

tration, creating a character, imagination and focus.

This exercise can be done alone or in a group.

minutes.

chair placed in front of an audience.

How to: The class sit down as an audience with a chair centre stage in front of them. Ask a volunteer to sit on this chair and to do nothing while sitting on the chair. The volunteer may look awkward or apologetic, or they may try to entertain, but encourage the student to do nothing. After a minute or two, the teacher walks over to the person sitting on the chair and whispers a purpose in their ear. The purpose might be that they are waiting for an appointment at the dentist, or that they are waiting for an exam to begin, or that they are resting because they have an injured ankle. The student will instantly look less awkward when they have a purpose and they will become more charismatic to the audience. Allow them to sit on the chair with a purpose for a minute or two and then relieve them and ask them to go and sit with the rest of the group. The teacher now explains that the actor must always have purpose while on stage or screen. Whether they are speaking dialogue, doing an activity or apparently doing nothing (just sitting on a chair), purpose should always be performed.

Now ask the students to come up one at a time and to sit on the chair with a purpose for 30 seconds to a minute. Give examples of purposes for the class to start with. Perhaps they are sitting in the park waiting for a friend they haven't seen in a while, or they are sitting to rest in an armchair after a difficult day at work, or they are sitting waiting for an audition. Props are not allowed. This is an exercise where the actor is laid bare with only themselves and an internal purpose to draw the audience in. This is a vulnerable position for the actor to be in as there is no dialogue or props to hide behind, but it's good to get used to from an early age.

Variation: This can also be performed as a group. Use chairs to set up a public space such as a train station, airport or cafe and explain to students that they are going to enter the space and sit down in silence but with a purpose. If, for example, the cafe were chosen, the class would come and sit down in the cafe on their own with a purpose. Examples of a purpose include to wait for a friend, to write a poem, to get warm as it's snowing outside or to rest a bad leg. Have half the class come and sit down in the cafe with a purpose, while the other half of the class watch. Then after about 5 minutes, swap over. Ask students to discuss what they noticed.

Tip: This is a silent acting exercise, and students should not be tempted into performing an overdramatic piece of mime.

The aim: To teach students that purpose on stage is necessary and must be added by the actor or director when it's not in the text or dialogue. Also to show students that they should never just stand or sit on stage without knowing why they are there.

10.2 Yes, let's, with inner motives

A fun warm-up exercise that encourages students to act out the internal motivations as well as the action.

Age: 8 plus.

Skills: Imagination, spontaneity and energy.

Participants: This exercise can be done alone or in a group.

Time: 10–15 minutes.

You'll need: A space big enough for the class to move about in.

How to: Students find a space in the room and are given an external action. For example, the teacher says, 'Bake a cake', and they say, 'Yes, let's' and perform baking a cake. Next, they are asked to bake a cake but to add an internal action as well, for example, bake a cake for your best friend who you've had an argument with. Or bake a cake for a baking competition you are determined to win. Students say, 'Yes, let's' and bake a cake with an internal action. They will instantly feel the difference between the two performances of baking a cake with an internal action and without. Here are some examples to work with.

- Build a fire.
- (With an inner motive) Build a fire as if you are lost in the woods in the hope the smoke might bring you help.
- Wash the car.
- (With an inner motive) Wash the car for your mum and dad as they are both sick in bed with the flu.
- Brush your teeth.
- (With an inner motive) Brush your teeth just before you go to the dentist.

Ask the students to also come up with some of their own ideas, which they can share with the class.

Variation: It's possible to add one of these inner motives to an improvisation scene to bring it to life. 'Park bench' (Chapter 8) works particularly well for this. You could have one person sat on the bench flossing their teeth as they are just about to go to the dentist and the other reading their notes as they have a history exam.

Tip: The simplest of actions are often the most effective such as brushing your hair, doing the washing up or cooking dinner. Students shouldn't feel compelled to come up with a unique action; however, they can be more imaginative with the inner motives if they wish.

The aim: To teach students that when an inner motive is given to an action, it makes a much stronger performance and adds dimensions.

10.3 Bringing attention to props and imagined surroundings

An exercise Konstantin Stanislavsky practises in *An Actor Prepares*, where the actor learns to give attention to objects.

Age: 8 plus.
Skills: Concentration, control, awareness, mindfulness, imagination and focus.
Participants: This exercise can be done alone or in a group.
Time: 10–15 minutes.
You'll need: A bag of props and perhaps some furniture that might be found in someone's surroundings, but avoid electronic devices such as phones and computers. Items might include a mug, a knitted scarf, a painting, a book, a candle, jewellery, a chair, a table and a piece of string. There needs to be at least one prop available for each student in the class.
How to: Students sit in a circle with all the props in the centre. Ask the students to take one prop and sit with it in the room somewhere. The teacher explains that in this exercise all the actor needs to do is give one prop their attention. However, this does not mean just holding a prop and looking at it; the aim is for the actor to really look at it and to focus their full concentration and attention on it. Now ask them to give the prop their full attention as if it were an item in a room they had just entered. The actor can touch the prop, examine it and move it about in their hands. The aim is for the student to have a natural relationship with this object. Now ask them to place this object in another part of the room, far away from themselves, and still to give it concentrated attention as if they are examining this prop from afar. Examining a prop from near and far is a great trick to use on stage in order to make a performance more naturalistic. When watching people in real life, you will often see their attention drawn to something of interest in the room, particularly in a new space.

Now set up a room on a stage with some chairs and props spread about it. It doesn't matter if this is a rather strange room with a bizarre collection of objects. Ask the students to sit down as an audience and ask for one volunteer to enter the stage and for them to concentrate on an object in the room. Encourage them to do this as naturally as possible without it feeling too forced; the best way to achieve this is for there to be genuine curiosity in the object. Leave the student on the stage for a minute or two concentrating on an object. They may find this very difficult as acting naturally with any audience is difficult; however, when practised, it becomes easier. Ask more volunteers to come up one at a time to practise this.
Variation: Give students a short scene to work with and ask them to as a team design the set for the scene. Ask them to imagine what furniture and props are in the room and to think about which objects their character might be drawn to. It's useful to use a scene where at least one of the characters is new to the surroundings. Let's use the scene below from *Great Expectations* as an example. One interpretation could

be that Miss Havisham is paying attention to a pack of playing cards on the table that she would like Pip and her daughter Estella to play with. And Pip's attention could be drawn to the cobwebs around the room as he is afraid of spiders.

Great Expectations

By Charles Dickens, adapted by Samantha Marsden.

Cast: Miss Havisham and Pip

Miss Havisham, a rich older lady dressed in every piece of jewellery she owns and an old wedding dress, has called for a poor boy, Pip, to come to her house.

Miss Havisham   Who is it?

Pip   Pip, ma'am.

Miss Havisham   Come nearer; let me look at you. Come close.

Pip goes in close, but doesn't look at her.

Miss Havisham   Look at me. You are not afraid of a woman who has not seen the sun since you were born?

Pip *(sounding afraid)*   No.

Miss Havisham puts her hands on her heart.

Miss Havisham   Do you know what I touch here?

Pip   Yes, ma'am.

Miss Havisham   What do I touch?

Pip   Your heart.

Miss Havisham   Broken!

Miss Havisham gives Pip a strange smile, then slowly takes her hands away from her heart.

Miss Havisham   I am tired. I want diversion, and I have done with men and women. Play. I sometimes have sick fancies. There, there! Play, play, play!

Pip looks around the room awkwardly.

Miss Havisham *(muttering)*   So new to him, so old to me; so strange to him, so familiar to me; so melancholy to both of us! Call Estella. Call Estella. You can do that. Call Estella. At the door.

Pip *(gets up and stands at the door)*   Estella. Estella.

Tip: Even if there are no props, ask students to use their imagination to create the surroundings and all the details within it.

The aim: To show students that bringing their attention to objects can create a naturalistic relationship between people and things on stage.

10.4 Know the condition and setting

An exercise where students add an imagined physical setting to the scene they are playing.

Age: 8 plus.

Skills: Imagination, awareness and creativity in response to the text.

Participants: This exercise can be practised alone or in a group depending on whether it's a monologue or a scene.

Time: 10–15 minutes.

You'll need: The students to already know a monologue or scene off by heart.

How to: Ask the students to consider a scene or monologue and to really think about where it is set and the details of it. Start with the question of where it is set physically, for example, in a bedroom, dining room, park or ice rink. Then ask them to think about the temperature, the smell, the objects around them, how private the space is, how safe the space is and so on. If, for example, I was playing Little Red Riding Hood and I was considering the scene where she meets the wolf for the first time, I know she is in the woods, but there are a lot of blanks I have to fill in to really make this scene believable. An example of one interpretation could be as follows:

> I'm in the forest in autumn; the leaves are falling and changing colour. It is a cold but bright day with a slight wind. I'm in the dense part of the forest at about the half way point between my own house and grandmother's house. Once I got a bit lost at this part of the journey before, but now I know these woods well. There are birds in the trees and squirrels busy collecting acorns. It is supposed to rain later so I hope to get back home before the weather changes. There is an earthy sweet smell in the air.

All of this detailed information about the setting is sure to change Little Red Riding Hood's behaviour. She may look up and track a falling leaf, for example, or kick some leaves, or giggle at a greedy squirrel, or a bad memory may flick through her mind as she passes the place where she once lost her way. She may adjust her hair as the breeze blows her hair into her eyes. She may breathe deeply as the air smells good.

The actor should always be aware of the details of their imagined surroundings. Surroundings have a big impact on our behaviour and the actor needs to have a good imagination for them.

Tip: It can be useful for actors to write down a description of the locations their characters perform in and even create physical mood boards or ones on the computer.

The aim: For the actor to imagine and respond to imagined surroundings.

10.5 Mood board and journals

A creative and academic exercise where students create journals, mood boards and playlists for their characters.

Age: 8 plus.

Skills: Building a character, literacy and analysis.

Participants: This exercise is for the student to practise alone.

Time: Up to several hours.

You'll need: A pen and paper and access to magazines and/or a computer.

How to (mood board): The actor takes a large piece of paper, or uses software on their computer, and creates a mood board for their character. Anything can be stuck onto this mood board so long as it seems to fit the character being played. The actor should choose things that remind them of their character and their character's tastes. Anything can be added to this board: pictures of clothes, furniture, animals, foods, places and anything else that the actor can think of. It can be useful to take this mood board into rehearsals and even hang it in a dressing room to remind the actor of the character's tastes.

How to (journal): The actor uses a journal or several pieces of paper and writes in it as if they are the character they are playing. They try to use the character's voice, describing things as the character would, seeing the world through their eyes. This can be done just once, but if the actor is feeling really dedicated, they can do this for a week or two, describing their day as their character would have seen it.

How to (playlists): Students design a playlist for their character and then listen to this in rehearsals and before performances.

Tip: Students should do this in a way they feel excited by; for some this might be through music, for others it might be through visuals and for others it may be through the written word. The students should choose their own way of connecting with a character.

The aim: For students to get to know their characters on a deeper level.

10.6 Actions with purpose

An exercise Konstantin Stanislavsky practises in *An Actor Prepares*, where the actor learns how to do an action with purpose.

Age: 10 plus.

Skills: Concentration, creating a character, imagination and focus.

Participants: This exercise can be done alone or in a group.

Time: 10–15 minutes.

You'll need: A door which can be opened and closed in the room.

How to: Ask the class to sit as an audience facing a door and ask one volunteer to close the door. Now ask the student to close the door again, but this time they imagine the reason behind this is because it's freezing outside and a cold draught is coming in. After the task has been performed, ask the class which was the more interesting way of closing the door, the first or second way. Most will agree that it is the second. Go on to explain that when an action has purpose, it makes it much more interesting to watch. One at a time let everyone in the class have a go at this exercise and give each student a purpose. Purposes for closing the door might include:

- It's freezing outside.
- The person has just had an argument with a person in the other room.
- There's a sleeping baby in the other room.
- The person has just said goodbye to their old school that they are leaving.
- The person wants some privacy in their bedroom to write a song they've had in their head all day.
- There's a violent rabid dog in the other room.

If it's a large class and the teacher doesn't have enough different ideas for closing the door, it's okay to give several students the same purpose.

Variation: Adding purpose in the above way can be done with many different activities other than closing the door. Different things can be played with, such as getting into a car, getting ready to go out or packing a bag. With added purpose, mundane activities become interesting to watch.

Tip: Remember the purpose has to be related to the action. For example, if the action were *to get in the car*, ask what is the purpose of getting in the car? Is it to go on holiday? To hospital? Or to escape a rabid lion?

The aim: For the actor to understand that purpose can be added to any activity and that when they do this, it instantly makes the performance more believable and interesting.

10.7 Adding history to a relationship

An improvisation exercise where two people bump into each other in the supermarket, but there is some history between them.

Age: 10 plus.

Skills: Improvisation, spontaneity and character building.

Participants: This exercise needs to be practised in pairs.

Time: 15–20 minutes.

You'll need: A space big enough for students to rehearse a sce...

How to: Ask the students to get into pairs and explain that they are both going
a character who is shopping. Ask them to think of at least one given circumstance
and one objective to help them create their character. For example, maybe one of
the characters is a poor law student at the nearby university (given circumstance)
and they are trying to stretch their weekly food shop as far as possible (objective).
The other person might be a mother and owner of a cafe (given circumstance)
and they need to buy lots of milk as the cafe has run out (objective). Once the
students have come up with a character each, both with one given circumstance
and one objective, together the pair can think up a past history between the two
characters. Perhaps the student used to work at the cafe but they got fired, or
the cafe owner is an old family friend who the student misses dearly, or the cafe
owner once caught this student stealing a piece of cake from the cafe.

After the given circumstances, objectives and piece of history have been
developed, ask the pair to start the improvisation. Once they've had 5 to 10
minutes to rehearse, ask them to share it with the rest of the class.

Variation: Adding a history between two characters can also be used in some
improvisation exercises. This can often result in comedy. Make sure the
two actors have a chance to agree their history first before they perform the
improvisation. Improvisation exercises which work well for this include: 'Taxi
driver with given circumstances' (Chapter 5), 'Broken-down lift' (Chapter 6), 'A
job interview' (Chapter 7) and 'Park bench' (Chapter 8).

Tip: The history between the characters can be either negative or positive.

The aim: For students to consider the history of a relationship between characters.

10.8 Character versus characterization

An academic exercise for students to use if they're playing a character; this can
help to create a polished performance.

Age: 11 plus.

Skills: Character building, literacy, imagination, social skills, life skills and analysis.

Participants: This exercise is practised alone.

Time: 15–20 minutes.

You'll need: The student will need to know a character from a play and/or book
very well to do this exercise. They will also need a pen and paper.

How to: Firstly, explain to students the difference between character and
characterization. Characterization is everything that can be observed and found
out about a person easily such as their age, job, gender, education, attitudes,

litics and personality. Character, however, is different; character refers to who a person really is under the surface. Character is not normally revealed until we see the choices a person makes under high pressure. For example, if a person is caught up in a natural disaster, say a terrible earthquake in the city, the audience will find out if they are generous (gives water to the injured) or greedy (loots a shop), if they are brave (helps get people out of the rumble despite tremors) or cowardly (runs away ignoring cries for help). Often characterization and character do not match; perhaps someone's characterization is brave and sporty, but under pressure their true character is cowardly.

Ask the students to consider a character they know well (preferably one they are working on for a performance) and to list all of their characterizations in one list and then their character in a list next to this. The list of characterizations is likely to be long and the character list may only have two or three words on it. But it is the character list that is most important to the actor as this reflects who the character truly is. Words that come up on the character list might include:

- Loving
- Cruel
- Loyal
- Traitor
- Brave
- Cowardly
- Honest
- Liar
- Determined
- Gives up easily
- Leader
- Follower
- Wise
- Closed-minded

Remind students that interpreting a character is a subjective business and that there is no right or wrong with this exercise. If I were playing Alice from *Alice in Wonderland*, for example, my lists might look something like this:

Alice's characterization

- 7-year-old girl
- Wealthy
- Lives in a big house in England

- Has a sister
- Likes order and stability
- Logical
- Curious
- Educated
- Confident
- Well mannered
- Rational
- Dignified

Alice's character

- Brave
- Determined
- Believes in justice

There are other ways to interpret Alice; this is just one example. Once students have listed their character's characterizations and character, encourage them to share it with the rest of the class. Then explain to them that they should read this list several times a day for a few days so as to internalize it in the hope that this will then shine through in their performance.

Tip: To find out a character's *true character*, look to the parts in the play where their underlying character is tested and see how they react.

The aim: For students to learn the difference between characterization and character and to apply this to a character they already know well.

10.9 Adding a contradiction

An academic exercise for students to use in order to develop a polished performance of a character.

Age: 11 plus.
Skills: Character building, literacy, imagination and analysis.
Participants: This exercise is practised alone.
Time: 15–20 minutes.
You'll need: The student will need to know a character from a play and/or book very well to do this exercise. They will also need a pen and paper.
How to: Explain to the students that all people have internal contradictions, particularly as they get older. To create a truly natural performance, the actor must know their character's internal contradictions; this is normally two (or

ore) objectives, feelings or given circumstances that clash. For Macbeth, for example, his internal contradiction is that he is ruthlessly ambitious, but he is also plagued by his conscience. It is the guilt that he feels that contradicts his actions, thus making his character interesting.

To make a character honest and natural, they must be full of internal contradictions. If the actor has the skill to play the contradictions on top of everything else (given circumstances, actions and objectives), they will fascinate and engage audiences. The advanced actor should not be aiming for three dimensional characters but for multidimensional characters. Characters should be riddled with internal conflict, for example:

> I want to be brave, but I don't want to stand up to that bully for fear she will hurt me and I don't want mum to see that I've been hurt at school again. But if I can be brave, the bully might stop and then my dad will be proud that I stuck up for myself. But I am a coward, I'm not brave, who am I kidding?

Here pride and lack of courage battle. It's these internal conflicts that we have within us that draw an audience in, move a story forwards and make an actor appear natural. The actor who can perform internal contradiction with authenticity is the actor who will mesmerize.

Ask the students to think about a character they have been working on for a while, one they know well, and then ask them to list this character's internal contradictions. If I were playing Jane from *Jane Eyre*, for example, my list might look something like this:

Jane's contradictions

- Wants to be looked after but wants autonomy.
- Committed to justice but feels she needs to fit into an unjust society.
- Wants love but also to be free (not easy for a woman in the Victorian period).

Tip: To find a character's internal contradictions, the student will need to study the whole play; it will have to be a well-written play as weaker writers tend not to develop the contradictions. Shakespeare and Dickens tend to write characters with many different contradictions within them, which is part of the reason these works are still used and loved today. When working with weaker scripts, the actor should develop the character and create the depth and contradictions themselves. On many TV and film sets, these days the actor plays a role in writing the character with the script writers so that the depth is there.

The aim: For students to explore their character's internal contradictions on a deep level.

10.10 Hiding a problem

An advanced acting exercise where students hide a problem.

Age: 12 plus.

Skills: Communication skills, improvisation, character building, ~p~ compassion and listening.

Participants: This exercise can be practised in pairs or in a group.

Time: 20–25 minutes.

You'll need: A chair, the students to know each other and a psychologically safe rehearsal space.

Note of caution: In this exercise, the students have to hide an imaginary problem; it is very important that this is an imaginary and not a real problem for the students acting this out.

How to: Students sit as an audience with a chair placed in front of them centre stage. The teacher explains that very often people try to hide certain information, and when acting it is this process of hiding information that can make a character more believable. For example, how often have you heard someone say they are 'fine', but their tone and delivery tell you they are not?

Ask a volunteer student to sit on the chair and explain to them that they are not to be themselves; they are to imagine a character. Ask them to give you this character's name; so if the student were called Salma in real life, maybe she'd choose to be a character called Trix. Salma can make Trix any character she likes, with a personality different from herself. Now Salma privately gives Trix a problem. This problem could be anything. Maybe Trix is being bullied at school, or she has an eating disorder, or it could be something minor such as she has a tummy ache. Salma can choose any problem she likes so long as it is suitable for the age group practising the exercise, and it's not a problem Salma has in her real life.

Now Salma sits on the chair in character as Trix, with students asking her lots of questions about her life. Salma can make up the answers on the spot to create Trix. Trix does not want anyone to know her problem; she wants to keep it a secret, while it's the audience's job to find out the problem. As such, the audience may ask some tricky questions, putting Trix on the spot. Trix can be affected by the questions, and her body language may well reflect something different from what she is actually saying. The audience might ask about Trix's home life, school, friends and eating habits, and they should be able to tell from the actor's body language when they are getting close to her problem. For example, if Trix chose the problem of being bullied at school, when asked if she likes school, she might look sad, curl into herself and say, 'Yes.' Once it seems the audience has found the problem, stop the exercise, ask them what they thought the problem was, and then ask Salma to reveal it.

Allow as many people as would like to practise this exercise to do it. It's often a very popular one with teenagers, so give the class plenty of time if it's a large group. It's fine if the same problem is used several times by different students as each will portray it differently. Do keep reminding students that they must not use a problem that is true to themselves. This is for two reasons: you do not want to trigger anything in them that a therapist would be better dealing with; nor do you want students to feel judged or that they are sharing real-life situations with the class.

Variation one: Ask the students to get into pairs and explain that they are going to create a short scene together. Both will have a problem to hide, but one will be super-chirpy and almost frantic about it, energetically pretending everything is fine, while the other will be more down and closed about their issue. The pair of them are sitting next to each other at a 'making friends' event their teacher has imposed on them, and they are trying to get to know each other, both hiding their problems in different ways. Once they've had 5 to 10 minutes to practise this scene, they can show it to the rest of the class, and the class can try to guess the two problems.

Variation two: A hidden problem can also be added to some improvisation exercises. Ones which work well for this include: 'Taxi driver with given circumstances' (Chapter 5), 'Broken-down lift' (Chapter 6), 'A job interview' (Chapter 7) and 'Park bench' (Chapter 8).

Tip: Body language can be a very useful tool to reveal the subtext.

The aim: To show students that acting isn't just about revealing; it's also about concealing.

11 BRINGING THE TEXT TO LIFE

Introduction

To bring the text to life, the actor must know their character's given circumstances, objectives, actions, relationships, character traits and contradictions. The more research and thought the actor gives to their character, the stronger the chances are of a convincing performance. However, even the most hard working students sometimes need a little help with bringing the text to life. Students who 'over-rehearse' run the risk of a dull and dry performance. In this chapter, I've provided some exercises to help pump some life back into a scene or monologue that's become stale.

One problem I've noticed with children and teenagers is that many suffer under the direction of an over-controlling drama teacher, particularly when it comes to exam pieces or drama school audition monologues. Some teachers tell students exactly when to stand up, when to lift their hand, when to look sad and so on. But this produces a robotic imitation of the drama teacher's interpretation of the piece, whereas believable acting comes from the actor's instincts. The good drama teacher should teach a student how to approach a piece, guiding the actor so that they can have their own interpretation of how their scene or monologue should be played. Bringing the text to life is about bringing the character to life within the actor.

11.1 Shaking up an over-rehearsed piece

An exercise where a well-rehearsed scene is shaken up, an activity often facilitated in the audition room by the audition panel.

Age: 8 plus.
Skills: Imagination, awareness and creativity in response to a text.
Participants: This exercise can be practised alone or in a group depending on whether it's a monologue or a scene.

minutes.

he students to already know a monologue or scene off by heart.

lents are working on a scene or monologue and it has become a little

ed, ask them to perform the piece, and while they are performing,

rent things for them to do. For example, 'find your car keys', 'make a cake' or 'cut your finger nails'. This may throw a student if they have become set in their ways, but throwing them is good; students should never get into the habit of robotically performing a piece. Performing should always be fresh, scary and unpredictable. This exercise is a great way to shake the actor up if they are performing on autopilot; it can open up the actor to play the character in a way they might not have before; in some cases, it can also distract them so that the emotion of the piece bubbles up from the inside unexpectedly. Once when I studied under a very talented acting coach, he asked me to perform my monologue while washing the dishes. This felt unnatural and strange to me at first as I was used to performing the piece in a set way. But to my surprise, half way through the monologue, real tears started rolling down my cheeks; washing the dishes somehow opened up a pathway that allowed the emotion of the piece to come through.

Adding direction such as washing the dishes, doing a balletic dance or jogging on the spot while doing a scripted piece is commonplace in the audition room. The audition panel give out bizarre directions like this to see if the actor can take direction without it stumping them. One friend of mine, who was auditioning for a film, was asked to perform his piece imagining that he was in an elevator that was filling with skittles.

Tip: Practise this exercise with students who are performing a scripted monologue for an exam or audition.

The aim: For students to practise how to be adaptable while performing a scripted piece.

11.2 Adding an internalized secret

A technique to help add subtext to the text.

Age: 8 plus.

Skills: Creating a character, improvisation and focus.

Participants: This can be practised alone if the piece is a monologue or as a cast if it's a scene or play.

Time: This varies depending on the length of the script.

You'll need: The students to know a scene or monologue off by heart.

How to: The teacher explains that the scene or monologue is going to be performed with an internalized secret. This could be physical: perhaps they have a headache, or they didn't sleep well last night, or they are feeling great as they have been practising yoga a lot recently. Or the secret could be psychological: perhaps

they have been feeling very down lately due to confiden[...]
very attracted to someone else in the scene but wouldn't [...]
know, or they are feeling guilty as they ate the remains of [...]
egg that he was saving.

Ask the students to perform with one physical o[...]
and see how that changes the performance of the scen[...]
this again but with a different secret. Ask them to try [...]
different ways and to see if any of the interpretations are beneficial; if they are,
they should keep them in.

Tip: Make the internalized secret one that the character is likely to have.

The aim: For students to explore adding extra subtext to a scene.

11.3 Getting to know the text

A written exercise where students get to know and analyse their scripts.

Age: 8 plus (if the students are confident readers).
Skills: Concentration, creating a character, critical thinking, literacy and analysis.
Participants: This exercise is practised alone.
Time: This is highly variable depending on the student and length of the script. It
may take several hours, days or weeks of private study.
You'll need: A scene or whole script and a pen (maybe some highlighters) and a
notebook per student.
How to:
Step one – the first read-through: When students first get their script, ask them to
read it all the way through in one sitting. This is a very exciting time; however,
be vigilant at this stage as slower readers may find reading aloud in front of a
group very stressful. Be quick to offer them help and support, and don't force
anyone to read out loud if it makes them feel uncomfortable. I'm dyslexic and
group read-throughs always filled me with terror! If possible, allow students to
have some time alone with a script before asking them to read it out loud. After
the first read-through, ask the students to jot down their initial responses to
the script and then share their responses with the rest of the class. Stanislavsky
believes the initial response to a first read-through is very important; encourage
students to cherish and reflect on their first read-through.
Step two – understanding the text: It's vital that the actor fully understands the
whole play and every word that they say. Many words may need explaining, or
looking up in the dictionary, especially with younger students. Allow students
to write down their own translations next to the original text if they wish. This
is particularly important when performing Shakespeare.
Step three – round-the-table analysis: This is where the rehearsal process
becomes collaborative and the actors and director sit down together around
a table to discuss the text. Ask the students to sit in a circle and to discuss the

...ts meaning, the characters and how it might be directed. Questions for ...cussion might include:

- What are the main events of the play?
- What are the characters' motives?
- What are the play's themes?
- When is the play set?
- What are the characters' given circumstances?
- At what point do the characters in the play change (if at all)?
- What are the characters' objectives?
- What are the characters' relationships?

Step four – list facts: Ask the students to do as much research into their characters as possible by reading the play and any other material about that character and the time the play is set in. Ask them to list as many facts as they can find out about their character; these will comprise some of the given circumstances.

Step five – create: Once the actor has taken everything they can from the writer and other research, they are free to add material and fill in the blanks and history of their character. Ask the students to list all the given circumstances, both those the writer has given and those the actor has created. Also ask the actor to write into the script all the character's objectives and actions.

Tip: Getting to know the text can be a lengthy but enjoyable process. The age and ability of the class will determine how much input the teacher will need to contribute during this process.

Aim: For students to fully get to know and understand the text they are working with.

11.4 Adding pauses

A challenge to students to add pauses into the script.

Age: 8 plus.

Skills: Concentration, literacy, timing, analysis and awareness.

Participants: This can be practised alone if the piece is a monologue or as a cast if it's a scene or play.

Time: This varies depending on the length of the script.

You'll need: For the students to know a scene or monologue well, plus each student will need a pen and a script to work with.

How to: The most common phrase I use when directing children and teenagers in script work is 'use your pauses'. Far too many young people are in a rush to get their lines out, as if they might forget them if they don't say them fast enough. So, first of all, encourage students to know their lines off by heart so that they don't have to worry about forgetting them. Then encourage them to add pauses into their script work. Explain that a pause will bring the audience in and that silence ... *(dramatic pause)* ... is one of the most powerful tools an actor has. Some students will have a good instinct for when to pause, and the teacher should praise this and encourage others to learn from it, while other students will struggle with pauses.

Ask the students to go through their scripts and write in all the pauses. The pause may be for a physical reason: the character stops to pour a drink perhaps. Or the pause may be triggered by a psychological reason: the character might be remembering something, or working out a problem, or they may be lost for words. Ask the students to write not only the pauses into their scripts but also the reasons why. If I were playing the monologue below from *Romeo and Juliet*, for example, I might write my pauses in as follows:

Juliet Farewell! [PAUSE: realize I may never see my nurse again.] God knows when we shall meet again.

I have a faint cold fear thrills through my veins,

That almost freezes up the heat of life: [PAUSE: dark thoughts and panic flick through my mind.]

I'll call them back again to comfort me:

Nurse! [PAUSE: listens for the nurse, but she doesn't come.] What should she do here?

My dismal scene I needs must act alone. [PAUSE: picks up the vial and inspects it.]

Come, vial.

What if this mixture do not work at all?

Shall I be married then to-morrow morning?

No, no: this shall forbid it: lie thou there. [PAUSE: as she considers how she might stab herself with the dagger, where in the body? How much will it hurt?]

Laying down her dagger.

What if it be a poison, which the friar

Subtly hath minister'd to have me dead,

Lest in this marriage he should be dishonour'd,

Because he married me before to Romeo?

I fear it is: and yet, methinks, it should not

For he hath still been tried a holy man.

How if, when I am laid into the tomb,

I wake before the time that Romeo

Come to redeem me? there's a fearful point!

Shall I not, then, be stifled in the vault

To whose foul mouth no healthsome air breathes in,

And there die strangled ere my Romeo comes?

Once students have added their pauses and the reasons why, ask them to perform the scene or monologue to the class in this way, and if any of the pauses don't feel right during the performance, they should be cut.

Tip: Some characters will pause more than others. Wise characters, for example, may pause more than characters who are always in a rush.

The aim: To encourage students to use their pauses for dramatic effect.

11.5 Letting the subconscious take over

The ultimate aim for any actor!

Age: 8 plus.
Skills: Imagination, confidence, becoming a character and trust.
Participants: This is obtained alone.
Time: Not applicable.
You'll need: The actor to have done all of their research and to be open and confident to handing over their performance to the subconscious.
How to: The best actors will do all the ground work: learn their lines, understand the text, and know their given circumstances, their objectives, their actions, and the inner and outer workings of their characters. Then the final step is for the actor to be brave enough to let their subconscious mind take over. The background preparation is the actor's springboard to dive into a truthful performance where the actor forgets themselves and fully becomes the character they are performing. It takes a brave artist to delve into the subconscious, but this ultimately is where true art lies. The subconscious is somewhere every drama teacher should encourage their students to go. Ask students to work on a scene that they have been working on for a while. Once they know all of the given circumstances, actions and objectives, then ask them to perform it without thinking of any of that. Encourage them to perform the scene as if no one is watching.

Tip: Do a relaxation exercise before this, and maybe even encourage students to listen to a piece of music that gets them into character.

The aim: For students to be able to perform from a subconscious place and deliver an authentic and truthful piece of acting.

11.6 Adding beats

A written exercise where students add beats into a script.

Age: 10 plus.

Skills: Concentration, critical thinking, literacy, analysis and focus.

Participants: This can be practised alone if the piece is a monologue or as a cast if it's a scene or play.

Time: This varies depending on the length of the script.

You'll need: For the students to know a scene or monologue well, plus each student will need a pen and a script to work with.

How to: Many facilitators, actors and directors will have varying opinions on what constitutes a beat; here I have taken just one of many interpretations. Adding beats to the text is an excellent way to break it up. One of the worst things that can happen to a scripted performance is for it to become a monotone drawl with no changes in it. Beats are a way of punctuating acting. A new beat occurs when:

- An actor changes to a new action.

- An actor changes their objective.

- There is an exit or entrance.

- There is a change in conversation.

- There is a new physical activity.

- There is a change in emotion.

Some people mistakenly think that beats are somewhere you add a pause, but this is not the case. A beat indicates that the actor changes their performance in some way. It's important to add beats throughout the text and to note not only the beat but also the change in action, emotion and/or objective. How one applies beats to a script is subjective, but if I were playing Miss Havisham from *Great Expectations* in the scene below, here's how I might interpret the beats (added in square brackets):

Great Expectations

By Charles Dickens, adapted by Samantha Marsden.

Cast: Miss Havisham and Estella

Estella is Miss Havisham's adopted daughter. Miss Havisham is a very manipulative old lady who has treated Estella like a doll and used Estella as a pawn in her games.

Miss Havisham and Estella are sitting together, arms linked, Miss Havisham holding onto Estella's hand. Estella slowly pulls herself away.

Miss Havisham   [BEAT challenge (action), find out what's wrong with Estella (objective), distressed (emotion)] What! Are you tired of me?

Estella   Only a little tired of myself. *(She stands up and looks at the fireplace.)*

Miss Havisham   Speak the truth, you ungrateful girl. [BEAT trigger (action), make Estella listen (objective), frustrated (emotion)] *(Hits her stick on the floor.)* You are tired of me.

Estella stays calm, not reacting to her anger.

Miss Havisham   [BEAT insult (action), make her tell me what's wrong (objective), aggressive (emotion)] You stock and stone! You cold, cold heart.

Estella   What? You blame me for being cold? You?

Miss Havisham   Are you not?

Estella   You should know. I am what you have made me. Take all the praise, take all the blame, take all the success, take all the failure; in short, take me.

Miss Havisham   [BEAT shame (action), make Estella feel guilty (objective), wronged (emotion)] Look at you! So hard and thankless. I have spoilt you, given you years of kindness.

Estella   You have been very good to me, and I owe everything to you. What do you want?

Miss Havisham   Love.

Estella   You are my mother by adoption. I have said that I owe everything to you. All I possess is freely yours. Beyond that, I have nothing. I cannot give you what you never gave me.

Miss Havisham   You say I never gave you love! Did I never give you burning love? [BEAT provoke (action), control what Estella is saying (objective), bitter (emotion)] Call me mad, call me mad!

Estella   Why should I call you mad. I, of all people? Does anyone live who knows what set purposes you have as well as I do? I have learned from you and looked up into your face, even when your face was strange and frightened me!

Miss Havisham [BEAT hearten (action), make Estella love me (objective), rejected (emotion)] So hard, so hard!

Estella Who taught me to be hard?

Miss Havisham [BEAT scare (action), make Estella say that she loves me (objective), distraught (emotion)] But to be hard on me! Estella, Estella, to be hard to me!

A pause as Estella looks at Miss Havisham calmly.

Estella I cannot think why you should be so unreasonable. I have never been unfaithful to you, or your schooling. I have never shown any weakness.

Once students have added their beats, emotions, actions and objectives, ask them to perform the scene in this way. Encourage them to experiment with what works and what doesn't and to change beats, actions, objectives and emotions until they work.

Tip: Working on a script in this way can be very helpful for some students but unhelpful for others. The teacher should teach students this practice but not enforce it as a way to work on the text for those whom it does not help.

The aim: For students to use beats in the script they are working on so as to break the scene up and give a more dynamic performance.

11.7 Immediacy

An exercise similar to one Uta Hagen teaches, where immediacy is added to a scene by having the actor search for an object.

Age: 10 plus.

Skills: Concentration, creativity, spatial awareness and spontaneity.

Participants: This can be practised alone if the piece is a monologue or as a cast if it's a scene or play.

Time: This varies depending on the length of the script.

You'll need: The students to know a scene or monologue well.

How to: Ask the actor to perform a scripted scene that they know well and to act out this scene while trying to find an object on the stage. This object should be something the character might conceivably need to find – a jumper perhaps, or car keys, or a lost earring. Ask the actor to play the whole scene or monologue while looking for the object. If there are several actors on stage at the same time, only have one of them looking for an object; otherwise it may become a little too chaotic.

Tip: It can be fun to actually hide an object from the actor and have them find it.

The aim: To add some life and immediacy into the scene.

11.8 Connecting to the emotion of a piece

An exercise to help students connect to the emotion of a piece.

Age: 11 plus, or 8 plus, for students who are mature for their age.

Skills: Emotional intelligence, life skills, literacy, analysis and compassion.

Participants: This can be practised alone if the piece is a monologue or as a cast if it's a scene or play.

Time: This varies depending on the length of the script but probably several hours.

You'll need: For the students to know a scene or monologue well, and each student will need a pen and script to work with.

How to: In my opinion, connecting to the emotion of a piece is the number-one thing an actor can do to improve their performance. However, it is also one of the hardest things to do as it takes courage. Some actors don't even need to think about how to add emotion to a piece; they just do it instantly and naturally, and for these actors, this exercise is probably no use to them. However, most actors need a little prompting and guidance, and this exercise will hopefully be of use to these actors.

Ask the students to sit down with their scripts and a pen and to write down every emotion their character is feeling throughout the play. This could be done on a line by line basis, word by word or scene by scene, depending on how changeable a character's emotions are. What a character is feeling is subjective, so explain to the students that this is their interpretation, no one else's, and they can interpret the character's feelings however they like. It's a good idea to give students a list of emotions so they have something to work with; below is a list to get them started:

Negative feelings: Lost, unsure, uneasy, stressed, irritated, enraged, hateful, aggressive, bitter, frustrated, resentful, disgusted, furious, reactive, short-tempered, sad, grumpy, sick, impatient, jealous, angry, revengeful, envious, disappointed, ashamed, afraid, powerless, diminished, guilty, dissatisfied, miserable, sulky, low, desperate, alienated, pessimistic, dejected, self-critical, self-deprecating, disheartened, despondent, stuck, blocked, despairing, hopeless, morose, reckless, burdened, trapped, negative, doubtful, uncertain, shy, disillusioned, distrustful, uncomfortable, disdainful, manipulative, judgemental, argumentative, distracted, disoriented, awkward, defensive, incapable, alone, paralysed, fatigued, useless, inferior, empty, distressed, pathetic, self-hating, distraught, broken, doomed, overwhelmed, trapped, weak, bored, disinterested, fearful, terrified, suspicious, tired, anxious, nervous, scared, worried, frightened, icy, rigid, restless, threatened, cowardly, insecure, defensive, dreadful, guarded, intimidated, paranoid, reckless, self-conscious, crushed, tormented, numb, deprived, pained, rejected, offended, heartbroken, appalled, wronged, humiliated, tearful, sorrowful, grieved, dismayed, remorseful, sullen, superior, unworthy, fragile, disconnected, devastated, blindsided, discontented, attacked, fake, shallow, indecisive, perplexed, embarrassed, hesitant, suspicious and obsessive.

Positive feelings: Comfortable, encouraged, surprised, understanding, interested, satisfied, accepting, kind, empathetic, tolerant, happy, friendly, present, affectionate, sensitive, brave, tender, attracted, passionate, admiring, warm, loved, compassionate, allowing, non-judgemental, appreciative, respectful, humble, gracious, patient, expansive, kindly, alive, blissful, joyous, delighted, overjoyed, festive, ecstatic, cheerful, elated, fun-loving, beautiful, light-hearted, easy-going, mellow, certain, child-like, uplifted, gratified, intrigued, absorbed, inquisitive, rested, curious, amazed, attentive, observant, amused, thoughtful, courteous, focused, humorous, playful, courageous, energetic, liberated, giving, optimistic, thrilled, intelligent, exhilarated, excited, alert, communicative, spunky, vigorous, tickled, eager, keen, earnest, inspired, enthusiastic, whole, daring, hopeful, upbeat, creative, constructive, helpful, motivated, productive, responsive, confident, free, sympathetic, conscientious, honoured, calm, content, quiet, serene, assured, clear, balanced, grateful, carefree, adequate, authentic, forgiving, sincere, reliable, euphoric, hardy, secure, honest, self-affirming, supportive, solid, glowing, radiant, reflective, grounded, open-minded, non-controlling, unassuming, trusting, supported, light, spontaneous, aware, healthy, meditative, graceful and natural.

If I were playing Sara in *The Little Princess*, for example, this is how I might interpret this scene (emotions added in the brackets):

A Little Princess

Written by Frances Hodgson Burnett, adapted by Samantha Marsden.

Cast: Ermengarde and Sara

Sara and Ermengarde live in a children's home. Sara is new and very rich.

Sara is crying.

Ermengarde   Are you okay? Are you in pain?

Sara   Yes. But the pain is not in my body. [Anxious] Do you love your father more than anything else in the whole world? [Lost]

Ermengarde   I hardly ever see him. He's always in the library reading things.

Sara   I love my father more than all the world 10 times over. [Tearful] That is what my pain is. He has gone away. [Heartbroken]

Ermengarde   Don't cry. It's okay.

The girls hug.

Sara   I'm okay. I promised my father I would bear it. And I will. [Graceful] You have to bear things. [Composed]

Ermengarde   I loved the story you told us all this morning.

Sara   Telling stories helps me bear it better. [Positive]

Ermengarde   Lavina and Jessie are best friends. I wish we could be best friends. Would you have me for yours? You're clever, and I know I'm the stupidest child in the whole school, but I – oh, I do so like you.

Sara   You are not stupid. Yes. We will be friends. [Warm] And I tell you what, I can help you with your French lessons. [Generous]

Ermengarde   Thank you.

The girls hug again.

Now ask the students to perform the script with these added emotions.

Variation: It can also be useful to bring emotion into an improvisation. Ask students to choose one or two emotions and then to play that throughout an improvisation. Improvisation exercises which work well for this include: 'I'm sorry I …' and 'I got you this present' (Chapter 4), 'Taxi driver with given circumstances' (Chapter 5), 'Broken-down lift' (Chapter 6), 'Hospital queue' and 'A job interview' (Chapter 7), and 'Park bench' (Chapter 8).

Tip: Although it might be tempting, it's best not to ask students under the age of 18 to remember a time they felt negative emotions and then to apply this as this could end up being emotionally traumatic for some. However, you can ask students to remember a time they felt positive emotions and then to apply that.

The aim: To help improve students' emotional intelligence and compassion and for that to help them with their performances.

SKILLS INDEX

A cross-referenced index of the exercises within this book is provided here, ordered by skill to aid the teacher in planning lessons.

Analysis

- Adding actions to a script
- Character versus characterization
- Adding a contradiction
- Knowing the condition and setting
- Getting to know the text
- Connecting to the emotion of a piece
- Adding beats
- Adding pauses

Acceptance

- The repetition exercise

Audition skills

- Entering an audition

Awareness

- Releasing tension while lying down
- A seated relaxation exercise
- Awareness of energy
- Counting to twenty
- Meditation

- Circles of attention
- Relaxation and breathing exercise
- Vocal forest
- Shaking hands with actions
- The smell exercise
- The five senses
- Imaginary objects
- Physical habits
- Exploring how props and costume affect movement
- Takeaway words
- Adding tension to create character
- Bringing attention to props and imagined surroundings
- Knowing the condition and setting
- Shaking up an over-rehearsed piece
- Adding pauses

Breathing and voice

- Relaxation and breathing exercise

Character building

- Hot-seating with given circumstances
- Creating given circumstances for fairy-tale characters
- Improvising scenes from a character's past
- Adding objectives to a scene
- Adding a need
- If I were a …
- Physical habits
- Body language for an interview
- Playing with eye contact
- Hiding a problem
- Adding history to a relationship
- Character versus characterization
- Adding a contradiction

Charisma

- Meditation
- Entering the stage
- Circles of attention

Concentration

- Releasing tension while lying down
- A seated relaxation exercise
- Awareness of energy
- Counting to twenty
- Meditation
- Circles of attention
- Relaxation and breathing exercise
- The repetition exercise
- Conditioning forces
- The smell exercise
- The five senses
- Imaginary objects
- Fairy-tale mime
- Sitting on a chair with purpose
- Actions with purpose
- Bringing attention to props and imagined surroundings
- Getting to know the text
- Adding beats
- Adding pauses
- Immediacy
- Letting the subconscious take over

Confidence

- Name game
- Projection
- The repetition exercise

- What are you doing?
- Park bench
- Imagine you are …

Creating a character

- Favourite feature
- Hot-seating with given circumstances
- Creating given circumstances for fairy-tale characters
- Taxi driver with given circumstances
- Improvising scenes from a character's past
- Packing a bag with given circumstances
- Entering the stage
- Conditioning forces
- Broken-down lift
- Group improvisation with objectives
- Adding actions to a script
- The 'magic if'
- Changing the tempo
- Exploring how props and costume affect movement
- Takeaway words
- Adding tension to create character
- Sitting on a chair with purpose
- Actions with purpose
- Getting to know the text
- Adding an internalized secret

Creativity

- Hello, my name is …
- Lead with your …
- Exploring the centre of energy
- Animal dinner party
- Lie about how you got here

- If I were a ...
- The five senses
- Imaginary objects
- Physical habits

Critical thinking

- Adding actions to a script
- Getting to know the text
- Adding beats

Diction

- Diction and tongue twisters
- Pass the vowel

Empathy

- The 'magic if'
- Hiding a problem
- Adding history to a relationship
- Connecting to the emotion of a piece

Energy

- Pass the vowel
- Soundscape
- Name game
- Pass the shake
- Elbow to elbow
- What are you doing?
- Park bench
- Imagine you are ...
- Pairs
- Yes, let's, with inner motives

Focus

- Releasing tension while lying down
- A seated relaxation exercise
- Awareness of energy
- Counting to twenty
- Meditation
- Circles of attention
- Relaxation and breathing exercise
- Sausages
- Packing a bag with given circumstances
- Entering the stage
- If I were a …
- The smell exercise
- The five senses
- Imaginary objects
- Sitting on a chair with purpose
- Actions with purpose
- Bringing attention to props and imagined surroundings
- Adding an internalized secret
- Adding beats

Group awareness

- Circles of attention
- Animal dinner party
- Pass the shake
- Elbow to elbow
- Fairy-tale mime

Imagination

- Soundscape
- Good evening, Your Majesty
- Lead with your …

- Letting the subconscious take over

Improvisation

- I'm sorry I …
- I got you this present
- Freeze!
- Status
- Yes, let's
- Improvising scenes from a character's past
- Packing a bag with given circumstances
- Entering the stage
- Conditioning forces
- Broken-down lift
- The telephone call
- Group improvisation with objectives
- Improvising with an action
- Shaking hands with actions
- Hospital queue with actions
- Improvising an advert with actions
- The letter
- Park bench
- Story circle
- Imagine you are …
- The five senses

Intuition

- The repetition exercise
- Acting to music
- Hot-seating with given circumstances
- Taxi driver with given circumstances
- The objective/obstacle exercise
- Why are you doing that?
- Broken-down lift

- The telephone call
- Objectives with props
- Changing the action

Lateral thinking

- Objectives with props

Life skills

- A job interview with actions
- Improvising an advert with actions
- Body language for an interview
- Playing with eye contact
- Character versus characterization
- Connecting to the emotion of a piece

Listening

- Pass the vowel
- Good evening, Your Majesty
- The repetition exercise
- Acting to music
- I'm sorry I …
- I got you this present
- Freeze!
- Lie about how you got here
- Sausages
- Hot-seating with given circumstances
- Taxi driver with given circumstances
- The objective/obstacle exercise
- Changing the action
- Improvising with an action
- What are you doing?
- Imagine you are …
- Hiding a problem

- Counting to twenty
- Name game
- Hello, my name is …
- Status
- Yes, let's
- Park bench
- If I were a …
- Story circle

Literacy

- Adding objectives to a scene
- Adding a need
- Adding actions to a script
- Takeaway words
- Character versus characterization
- Adding a contradiction
- Getting to know the text
- Connecting to the emotion of a piece
- Adding pauses

Mime

- Lead with your …
- Favourite feature
- Packing a bag with given circumstances
- Pairs
- Fairy-tale mime

Mindfulness

- Releasing tension while lying down
- A seated relaxation exercise
- Counting to twenty
- Meditation
- Exploring the centre of energy

- Bringing attention to props and imagined surroundings

Movement

- Awareness of energy
- Counting to twenty
- Lead with your …
- Exploring the centre of energy
- Animal movement
- Entering an audition
- Favourite feature
- Pass the shake
- Elbow to elbow
- Physical habits
- Changing the tempo
- Fairy-tale mime
- Exploring how props and costume affect movement
- Body language for an interview
- Playing with eye contact
- Adding tension to create character

Persuasion

- The objective/obstacle exercise
- The telephone call
- Objectives with props
- Changing the action

Projection

- Diction and tongue twisters
- Pass the vowel
- Soundscape
- Name game
- Vocal forest

- Hello, my name is …
- Good evening, Your Majesty
- Projection

Relaxation

- Releasing tension while lying down
- A seated relaxation exercise
- Awareness of energy
- Relaxation and breathing exercise

Social skills

- Hello, my name is …
- Animal dinner party
- Entering an audition
- Status
- Objectives with props
- Shaking hands with actions
- Hospital queue with actions
- A job interview with actions
- Park bench
- The 'magic if'
- Pairs
- Body language for an interview
- Playing with eye contact
- Hiding a problem
- Character versus characterization

Spontaneity

- Name game
- Vocal forest
- The song exercise
- The repetition exercise
- Acting to music

- I'm sorry I …
- I got you this present
- Freeze!
- Status
- Yes, let's
- Hot-seating with given circumstances
- Creating given circumstances for fairy-tale characters
- Taxi driver with given circumstances
- Conditioning forces
- The objective/obstacle exercise
- Why are you doing that?
- Broken-down lift
- The telephone call
- Changing the action
- Improvising with an action
- Hospital queue with actions
- A job interview with actions
- The letter
- What are you doing?
- Park bench
- If I were a …
- Story circle
- Imagine you are …
- The 'magic if'
- Yes, let's, with inner motives
- Hiding a problem
- Adding history to a relationship
- Shaking up an over-rehearsed piece
- Immediacy

Storytelling

- Freeze!
- Lie about how you got here

- Soundscape
- Name game
- Vocal forest
- Hello, my name is …
- Good evening, Your Majesty
- Projection
- The song exercise

GLOSSARY

Actions Actions refer to the things that a character does in order to achieve their objective. For example, a teenager may amuse, annoy, enchant or persuade a parent to lend them the family car.

Beat A beat is a way of breaking up the text. A new beat indicates that the actor changes their performance in some way. A new beat occurs when the previous subject matter, action, emotion, objective or physical activity changes.

Block When the movements are set for the actors on the stage or in relation to the set.

Character A person portrayed by an actor.

Conditioning forces A phrase Uta Hagen coined in her book, *Respect for Acting*. Conditioning forces influence a person's behaviour such as being in a hurry, or in the dark, or being cold, hot, nauseous or hungry.

Duologue A part in the script with speaking roles for two actors.

Emotional recall A technique central to method acting whereby the actor recalls memories and then applies these feelings to the character they are playing.

Fourth wall An imagined wall between the performers and audience.

Given circumstances The term 'given circumstances' was coined by Konstantin Stanislavsky. This refers to the environmental, historical and situational conditions a character finds himself or herself in.

Improvisation Where a scene is created spontaneously without the use of a script.

Intuition To use one's instincts over conscious reasoning.

Lateral thinking An approach to a situation, or problem, from a new and perhaps even unexpected angle.

Literacy The ability to read and write.

Mindfulness A mental state where one lives in the moment and is alert and awake.

Mime A technique whereby the performer communicates action, character and emotion through gesture, expression and movement without the use of words.

Monologue A speech delivered by one character; normally the text is at least five sentences.

Objective All of the character's wants and needs.

Obstacle Something that stands in the way of a character's objective.

Physicalizing Expressing one's emotions, given circumstances, actions and objectives in a physical way.

Props Objects used in theatre or on set to help tell the story.

Safe space A safe space is an environment where students know they will be accepted for who they are and a place where they feel free to experiment creatively.

Spontaneity   In a state of being able to follow impulses.

Status   The position of one individual in relation to another, often relating to social or professional standing.

Subconscious   A part of the mind that the individual isn't fully aware of but which influences actions, emotions and physicalization.

Text   A piece of writing.

Verbal reasoning   The ability to reason and persuade by using concepts expressed through words.

BIBLIOGRAPHY

Uta Hagen with Haskel Frankel, *Respect for Acting* (New Jersey and Canada: John Wiley and Sons, Inc., 1973).

Constantin Stansislavski, *An Actor Prepares* (Great Britain: Geoffrey Bles Ltd., 1973; Bloomsbury Academic, 2013).

INDEX

improvisation. *See* Skills Index
intuition. *See* Skills Index

journaling 127

lateral thinking. *See* Skills Index
listening. *See* Skills Index
literacy. *See* Skills Index
loosening up. *See* warm-ups

meditation 6–7, 11–12
Meisner, Sanford
    the repetition exercise 50–1
memory exercises 70–2, 100–2
    affective memory exercises 2, 100–2
method acting 2, 28–9, 100–2
mime. *See* Skills Index
mindfulness. *See* Skills Index
monologues, working on 34–5, 39–40,
    60–1, 78, 100–2, 135, 138–9
    practicing alone 119–20, 126–7,
    135–6
mood boards 127
motivations 74–6, 123
movement. *See* Skills Index

objectives 15, 57, 65–76, 77–8, 93–5, 105,
    128–9, 135, 137–8, 140–3
obstacles 54, 70–2, 82

patience 10
persuasion. *See* Skills Index
physicality. *See* body language
professionalism 39–40
projection. *See* Skills Index
props, working with 35, 47–8, 69–70,
    92–3, 97, 100, 111–12, 124–6

relaxation. *See* Skills Index
releasing inhibitions 21–2, 31, 39–40
releasing tension. *See* relaxation

safe space 2–3, 50–1, 121
script, working with a 13–15, 72–7, 84–7,
    107–10, 124–6, 131–2, 135–46
self-control 42–3
Shakespeare, William 78, 132, 137
    Macbeth 132
    Romeo and Juliet 61, 72–4, 101–2,
    139–40
social skills. *See* Skills Index
spatial awareness 33
speech 19–22
spontaneity. *See* Skills Index
Stanislavsky, Konstantin 137
    An Actor Prepares 89, 121–2, 124–8
    circles of attention 12–15
    given circumstances 53–63, 66–8, 78,
    93–4, 99–100, 105, 128–9, 135,
    137–8, 140–1
    magic if 54, 89, 99–100
storytelling. *See* Skills Index
Strasberg, Lee
    creative concentration 102–3
subconscious 41, 53, 89, 140–1
subtext 78–9, 81–2, 105, 133–4, 136–7

teamwork. *See* Skills Index
tension, added to character 114–17
text work. *See* script
timing 138–40
tongue twisters 19–21
trust. *See* Skills Index

unblocking. *See* relaxation

verbal reasoning. *See* Skills Index
voice. *See* Skills Index
    vocal hygiene 26–8

warm-ups 5–15, 17–29, 31–6, 41–7, 78,
    90–1, 97, 105–7, 123
Wizard of Oz, The 65